THE GREAT WAY FOR THE THIRD

UNIVERSAL SALVATION

MAKE OF YOURSELF A LIGHT

THIỆN QUANG

Translated by
DIỆU ĐỨC

Cao-Dai Temple Overseas
2017

Content Editor and Cover Designer:
Bri Bruce Productions

ISBN 978-0-9971367-2-2

In memory of

THIỆN QUANG (VÕ THÀNH VĂN)

Introduction

Throughout the world, humans are distressed by natural calamities and epidemics. In addition, their lives are also impacted by imminent wars caused by the discord that crushes fraternity and sparks extermination. Facing such atrocities and horrors, quite a few people wish to escape from this world and/or find some way to free themselves from these scourges.

Cao Dai teaching points out an unfailing and straightforward approach to turn this dreary time in the history of mankind into a new and brighter future. To build a happy world, there should first be happy people. With respect to human beings, happiness is essentially an emotion, i.e., a state of the inner rather than a factor from the outside (in *Happiness in Caodaist Conception*). Cao Dai teaching affirms that every human being has the intrinsic capacity to liberate his/her inner from the outside disturbances (in *Make of Yourself a Light*). And Caodaists should be the first to make that statement a reality and to serve examples for other people to join in the way of self-deliverance (in *How to Inaugurate the Great Way*).

How to validate the approach mentioned above? The answer is this: "A life of cultivation of deliverance can only be successful based on a life in harmony," (in *Make of Yourself a Light*). A person's life in harmony can be gauged via his/her fraternal interactions with other human beings based on the three standards: humaneness, peacefulness, and progress (in *The Spring in Human Fraternity*). A person's life in harmony should also be reflected through his/her ability of agreement with and/or adaptation to circumstances, exactly as the way newborns and young children live and grow (in *The Chorus between Spring Heart and Spring Scene*). Then how can an adult intentionally return to his/her newborn state and still be societally normal? He/she should distinguish and pursue the ethical happiness by controlling his/her desires and emotions (in *Happiness in Caodaist Conception*).

As Caodaists are expected to be the first to pave the way in this approach, they are also the first to access the new method of Cao Dai, namely the Triple Work method (in *Happiness in Caodaist Conception*), to exercise self-deliverance at all levels and aspects right in their current life. While acquiring their spiritual deliverance, they also contribute in making human society a better world through their practice of living in harmony.

We hope the readers find some inspiring ideas from this collection of brother Thiện Quang's seminars and speeches to shed some light on how to transform this troubling world into a peaceful and livable one.

Diệu Đức
On the Anniversary of
the Inauguration of the Great Way
Đinh Dậu year (2017)

About the Author and Translator

THIỆN QUANG (VÕ THÀNH VĂN) has been a Caodaist since 1980. He completed the training courses on Cao Dai teaching Level 1, Level 2, and the *Phó Ban* (Advanced Level) at Cơ Quan Phổ Thông Giáo Lý Đại Đạo (the Organization for Preaching the Doctrine of the Great Way), Ho Chi Minh City, Vietnam. He served in many important capacities at this organization since 1991 and accomplished quite a lot of major projects, including research papers, books, seminars, speeches, conference presentations, and papers, as well as dozens of poems, songs, and choruses on Cao Dai teaching.

He received his B.S. and M.S. degrees in physics from Ho Chi Minh City University of Science, an engineering degree in information technology from Ho Chi Minh City University of Technology, and a Ph.D. degree in physics from the Institute of Physics (Ha Noi, Vietnam). He started his teaching career in 2006 as a physics lecturer at the University of Science (Ho Chi Minh City, Vietnam) and remained at this position until his passing.

DIỆU ĐỨC (TRẦN ÁNH-TUYẾT) has been a Caodaist since 1983. She was one of the author's fellows in the training courses on Cao Dai teaching Level 1 and Level 2. She is a member of Cao Dai Temple Overseas in California, USA, and the translator of the holy scripture Cao Dai Great Way: The Grand Cycle of Esoteric Teaching (Cao Dai Temple Overseas, 2015).

She received an M.S. degree in chemistry from San Jose State University and a Ph.D. degree in chemistry from University of California Davis. She is currently a biochemistry and chemistry lecturer at San Jose State University, California.

Brother **THIỆN QUANG** delivered his seminar *Happiness in Caodaist Conception* at the Inter-Religion Conference on Sep. 28, 2013, held in Phanxicô Đa Kao Monastery, Vietnam.

Acknowledgments

Make of Yourself a Light is an English-translated version of the book *Tự Thắp Đuốc Mà Đi* (Tam Giáo Đồng Nguyên, 2014). The translator would like to thank brother Huệ Khải (Lê Anh Dũng), the editor and publisher of the book *Tự Thắp Đuốc Mà Đi,* for kindly providing her a soft copy of this book. She also thanks sister Diệu Nguyên (Đinh Thị Thanh Mai) for her timely responses to every request or need for the completion of this translated book. Many thanks are due to sisters Phan Thị Bảo Trân and Trần Ngọc Như Quỳnh for providing the author's photographs.

In addition, the translator extends her sincere thanks and appreciation to all members of Cao Dai Temple Overseas and Cơ Quan Phổ Thông Giáo Lý Đại Đạo (the Organization for Preaching the Doctrine of the Great Way), whose continuous support and encouragement help her stay focused on her religious duties and goals.

Contents

MAKE OF YOURSELF A LIGHT

On the occasion of annual Vesak,[1] Buddhists all around the world remember the Founding Master, who self-reliantly sought the way to deliverance and achieved the Buddhahood right on Earth. Via Caodaist séance on the eighth day of the fourth month of Canh Tuất year (1970), Sakyamuni Buddha taught:

> *Every year people around the world celebrate the birthday of your Master while the disciples commemorate it. And of course, remembering your Master is remembering the way to deliverance from the endless cycle of this world.* [2]

This is the advice for everyone who remembers Buddha: Address such remembrance to the way of deliverance, and not to Sakyamuni personally.

Would it make sense if we honored someone who humbled himself to escape from the common mentality in this world?

Would it help if we expressed personal cult to a being whose ego is completely eradicated?

That is absolutely nonsense and pointless, unless such praise or veneration really raises in ourselves an awareness, a motivation to follow the footsteps of that extraordinary being on the spiritual way to deliverance.

---

[1] The anniversary of Buddha's birthday.

[2] Đức Thích Ca Như Lai; Thánh thất Bình Hòa, Ngọ thời, the eighth day of the fourth month of Canh Tuất year (May 12, 1970).

When Prince Siddhartha was born, many Brahmin masters came to the royal palace and prophesied that the prince would become either a great emperor or a buddha.

At age 29, the then emperor-to-be Siddhartha decisively left all the extreme glory of a royal life to engage in the indigent life of an ascetic, begging for food to stay alive during his quest for the spiritual deliverance.

After six years of self-struggling with an extraordinary willpower, that mighty beggar discovered the way to self-deliverance. Concentrating in this way and relying on his own efforts, he self-enlightened and achieved the Buddhahood at age 35.

Forty-nine years later, when Sakyamuni Buddha was about to leave the world (to pass into the Nirvana), He gave mankind the following directive: *Make of yourself a light!* [3]

What is in this directive? It contains the everlasting principle of the spiritual deliverance.

1. HOW TO MAKE OF YOURSELF A LIGHT?

Close to the end of his worldly life, Sakyamuni Buddha questioned Ananda: *How to make of yourself a light?*

Then He Himself answered it: *Rely upon yourself, upon the Dharma,* [4] *do not depend upon anything else. ...*

---

[3] Kinh Du hành, Trường A-hàm (The Long Agamas scripture), vol. 1, page.121.

[4] Translator's note: The term Dharma has many translations. By combining the English meaning of these words: teachings, truths, facts and natural laws, then emphasizing the definition depending on the nature of the subject being discussed, one can usually understand the meaning of Dharma in each instance. For example, the meaning

After I leave the world, whoever can learn and cultivate exactly that way is the excellent cultivator.[5]

What does it mean to *Make of yourself a light,* and how to head up?

That light is the true heart (the spiritual heart) in humans.

To make a light is to enlighten the inner true heart. To make of yourself a light is to apply your own efforts to enlighten yourself, without relying on any external refuge. Only the wisdom gained from your own efforts can light up the way to your spiritual deliverance and attainment.

Moreover, the venerable Buddha also stated: *Let the Dharma be your refuge, seek no other refuge.* This message implies a very profound meaning: The true Dharma can only exist within oneself, and everything else is outside him/her.

Indeed, in the Degenerate Age of Dharma when the Third Universal Salvation[6] is opened to promote the true

---

of *Dharma* in the Triple Gem's "Buddha, Dharma and Sangha" includes all of these: teachings, truths, facts and natural laws. (Source: http://buddhismteacher.com/dharma.php).

[5] Kinh Du hành, Trường A-hàm (The Long Agamas scripture), vol. 1, pages.120-121.

[6] Translator's note: Caodaism has its own historical viewpoint to explain the historic progress of mankind, which can be divided into three eras: The First Era (about 4,300 years ago), the Second Era (lasted for 30 centuries, from 2000 B.C. to about 1000 A.C.), and the Third Era (from the 19th century to the present). At the end of each era, God disseminates the Way (the Dao) into this world to save mankind. The Great Way for the Third Universal Salvation was initiated when God founded Caodaism in South Vietnam in Bính Dần year (1926).

Dharma, divine beings[7] advice Caodaists to self-explore to find the true Dharma within.

Đức Quan Âm Bồ Tát taught:

On the way of learning and cultivating, the cultivator must steadfastly concentrate in the quest for the true Dharma. The true Dharma is not elsewhere in the universe or in heaven, but within oneself. Once a person attains the awakening state, the true Dharma reveals and immediately detaches from the self, and he/she beholds his/her Nature to become Buddha.[8]

Since the day the Great Way for the Third Universal Salvation was initiated, God and divine beings have spread so much blessing into this world in the forms of invocation, the grand amnesty, the divine beings' friendly communication and teaching. Such favor helped the religion develop quickly, but unfortunately it also made quite a few Caodaist disciples and dignitaries depend extensively on the invisible power.

Divine favor—regardless of how precious it is—remains the external power, i.e, it is outside oneself. Of course, divine beings would continue to directly support mankind at various levels and in multiple forms as Caodaism is still in its early stage. Yet, the principle of spiritual deliverance remains unchanged.

In Bính Thìn year (1976), Divine Mother Đức Vô Cực Từ Tôn started mentioning this principle as an

---

[7] Translator's note: 'Divine beings' is a general term to indicate all the buddhas, immortals, saints, and deities.

[8] Đức Quan Âm Bồ Tát; Cơ Quan Phổ Thông Giáo Lý, Tuất thời, the 15th day of the seventh month of Đinh Tỵ year (August 29, 1977).

unavoidable truth that everyone should face sooner or later: *Children, one day you will have to make of yourself a light!*[9]

That day came very soon. Only a short period after Divine Mother's reminder, Đức Giáo Tông Vô Vi Đại Đạo taught: *From now on, you should make of yourself a light.*[10]

Three years later He insisted: *It is time for you, brothers and all fellow members, to make of yourself a light on the way up to the end of your mission.*[11]

In fact, He had explained it two years earlier:

> *I, Humble Monk, have not come to you frequently because I want you to make of yourself a light, stick with your responsibilities, think earnestly of the salvation mechanism, and be serene and tranquil in the evolution of circumstances. Only in serenity and tranquillity you attain enlightenment to avoid straying.*[12]

Đức Lý Giáo Tông's statement forces us to accept the following truth: Regardless of the outflow of salvation favor and the guidance from divine beings, if we cannot maintain serenity and tranquillity in our own heart, the greater divine favor we receive, the more dependent we become and the more easily we stray away.

---

[9] Đức Vô Cực Từ Tôn; Vĩnh Nguyên Tự, Tuất thời, the 11th day of the 11th month of Bính Thìn year (December 31, 1976).

[10] Đức Giáo Tông Vô Vi Đại Đạo; Cơ Quan Phổ Thông Giáo Lý, Tuất thời, the 15th day of the second month of Đinh Tỵ year (April 03,1977).

[11] Đức Giáo Tông Vô Vi Đại Đạo; Cơ Quan Phổ Thông Giáo Lý, Hợi thời, the 14th day of the second month of Canh Thân year (March 30, 1980).

[12] Đức Giáo Tông Vô Vi Đại Đạo; Cơ Quan Phổ Thông Giáo Lý, Tuất thời, the 29th day of the 12th month of Mậu Ngọ year (January 27, 1979).

Many years after Divine Mother's reminder, on the Annual Meeting at the Organization for Preaching the Doctrine of the Great Way in Quý Hợi year (1983), God explained it again as follows:

> *Your Divine Mother Vô Cực Từ Tôn insisted that you, children,* **make of yourself a light**, *to prepare for the future when you no longer have external refuge and should rely on your own. Your inner is where I, your Master, reside. It is where your Master and divine beings will teach you. Indeed, you should maintain your heart in steady state to be able to enlighten the divine revelation.* [13]

The action of *Make of yourself a light* in God's explanation bears no difference from that of Sakyamuni Buddha over two thousand years ago. Rely on your own efforts, on your inner, and not on anything outside yourself, including the divine blessing. Someday, we will no longer be able to perceive this great favor via our physical senses—it does not mean there is no more of such favor— then our true heart would allow us the unique ability to enlighten the divine revelation.

Also, it should be noted that the principle *Make of yourself a light* implies another deep meaning: We should successfully manage the outside. What can help us do this? Strength? Trickery? Talent? How helpless these are! Experience of the enlightened beings from past to present indicates that we must forbear and persevere in the inner to have sufficient strength to manage the outside.

---

[13] Đức Ngọc Hoàng Thượng Đế; Cơ Quan Phổ Thông Giáo Lý, Hợi thời, the 15th day of the second month of Quý Hợi year (March 29, 1983).

Đức Quan Âm taught: *When it is time to rely on your own strength, try your best to persevere and self-control to manage the circumstances!* [14]

Therefore, perseverance and forbearance are the most important virtues making up the internal power for anyone who wants to self-enlighten his or her own wisdom.

2. MAKE OF YOUR BEING A LIGHT

At the end of the 1970s, the term *Make of your being a light* started displaying in the literature of Cao Dai teaching through the statement of Đức Bảo Pháp Huỳnh Chơn, when He was ordered by Đức Đông Phương Lão Tổ to come and guide in the Dharma of heart:

To be a cultivator on the Great Way seeking the original and everlasting nature, I, your Elder Brother, advice you to first **make of your being a light** *to perceive the ultimate objective of the Dharma of heart, so that you progress steadily on the cultivation way, and would not balk when being tempted by innumerable demonic hindrances and obstacles.* [15]

Đức Bảo Pháp Huỳnh Chơn also stated:

Divinely appointed fellows should note that every meditation session implies the significance of celestial mechanism on temporal way. As cultivators, all you need is **make of your being a**

---

[14] Đức Quan Âm Bồ Tát; Thánh thất Bình Hòa, Ngọ thời, the eighth day of the fourth month of Canh Tuất year (May 12, 1970).

[15] Đức Bảo Pháp Chơn Quân Huỳnh Chơn; Cơ Quan Phổ Thông Giáo Lý, Tuất thời, the first day of the fifth month of Đinh Tỵ year (June 17, 1977).

***light**, then everything else will occur smoothly. Divine beings always open arms to wait, but as human heart is filled with anger and ignorance, with bias and arrogance, with clinging to the self, they cannot reach the arms of divine beings.*[16]

What does it mean *to Make of your being a light*?

As divine beings use it in the metaphysic meaning of Western philosophy, the term *being* here means *the currently existing state*. When digging deeply into the philosophical content of this simple concept, we can find the outflow of the way to deliverance right inside the modern civilization of mankind.

Philosopher René Descartes (1596-1650) insisted that *being must pair up with consciousness*.[17] Only when there is an awakening of our own consciousness can everything related to us exist. If Descartes had had a chance to learn the new method of Cao Dai, he would have had to confess as follows. Any time he had sat in meditation, but his mind would have been freely wandering around and/or in the state of continuous drowsiness (falling asleep), he would not have been aware of his meditation practice, then that practice had not existed. Anyone in such state of meditation—regardless of the number of years in practice—is exactly like someone who never practices meditation.

According to philosopher Eric Edmund Husserl (1859-1938), *being* is the result of *intention*, i.e., of the

---

[16] Đức Bảo Pháp Chơn Quân Huỳnh Chơn; Cơ Quan Phổ Thông Giáo Lý, Tuất thời, the third day of the 11ᵗʰ month of Kỷ Mùi year (December 21, 1979).

[17] Thiện Quang, *Triết học Tây phương*, page 71 (unpublished).

consciousness-on-purpose.[18] If Husserl had also learned meditation and entered a Caodaist hall of meditation, he would have had to confess as follows. Even when he had been fully aware of his meditation practice—in a seemingly perfect meditation session, no mind wandering, no drowsiness—but if his consciousness had not concentrated intentionally in practicing the true Dharma, this meditation session would not have existed. It is because although he had been aware of it, his awareness would not have done intentionally. And nothing guarantees that a life of self-cultivation built on such meditation practice could culminate in the true spiritual attainment.

Therefore, if they had a chance to read the phrase *Make of your being a light* in the above holy teachings, Descartes would probably explain it as the self-enlightenment of one's own consciousness, whereas Husserl would assert that it is the self-enlightenment of one's own consciousness with a definite intention.

Both the consciousness of Descartes and the intention of Husserl belong to the concept of *heart* in the teaching of the Way. *Make of your being a light* means use one's own efforts to light up one's heart, without relying on anyone else, or depending on any power or awaiting any authority.

Buddhism calls it *enlighten the heart* to *see into one's own nature,*[19] i.e., only when you can light up your heart are you able to see into your own nature. That is the meaning of *Make of yourself a light.*

Stating that self-reliance is the principle of spiritual deliverance does not mean we should turn down the

---

[18] Thiện Quang, *Triết học Tây phương*, page 98 (unpublished).

[19] Translator's note: Refer to the Vietnamese text: *"minh tâm"* để *"kiến tánh"*

assistance needed for our evolution. The life that we are living is a school for us to learn the dogmas of real life. In this school, everyone must *learn the dogmas of the outside to shed light on the dogmas of the inner.* [20] Everyone can employ all the necessary means of the temporal world, but should not depend on them; instead, he/she should only rely upon his/her own and upon the true Dharma of his/her inner.

What does this mean? Among those who employ a borrowed tool, if this tool gets lost, those depending on that tool would badly suffer while those relying upon their own self would remain unaffected.

Understanding this basic principle of spiritual deliverance, we can understand why Đức Đông Phương Lão Tổ insisted as follows when He taught the method of the Way: *Borrow it to say, point it out to practice; but it is also impermanent. The true outcomes of the Way must be proved by the spiritual attainment. Listen!* [21]

3. THE SPIRITUAL DELIVERANCE MUST BE PROVED

Would it be possible for Caodaists nowadays to duplicate Sakyamuni Buddha's achievements in the past? In this Degenerate Era, would it be possible for anyone to attain the spiritual deliverance right on Earth when he/she is still alive, or must he/she wait until death, and then until

---

[20] Đức Bảo Pháp Chơn Quân Huỳnh Chơn; Cơ Quan Phổ Thông Giáo Lý, Tuất thời, the first day of the fifth month of Đinh Tỵ year (June 17, 1977).

[21] Đức Đông Phương Lão Tổ; Bát Nhã Tịnh Đường, Hợi thời, the 20th day of the fourth month of Quý Sửu year (May 22, 1973).

receiving God's favor to be able to enter the everlasting realm?

Based on the principle *Make of yourself a light*, we—rational human beings who are living and cultivating in this world—certainly should reject the latter case, as Đức Bồ Tát Quan Âm taught:

> *You should know that the way of deliverance can be applied everywhere. Deliverance from the stagnancy of selfish soul is to actively service and guide humans in this world. Deliverance from the somber of spirit is to willfully forge the heart, by following the true Dharma, until it becomes pristine and serene. Once everything is thorough with respect to the spiritual and temporal way, no need to regret or worry about defects; indeed, that is the deliverance in the ways of deliverance.* [22]

At all times, the Dharma of the Great Way requires the cultivator to self-cultivate and self-attain. Then, would it be possible to prove the outcomes of the deliverance right in this current life, instead of waiting until after death?

Đức Vạn Hạnh Thiền Sư taught:

> *No need to wait until death of the body to free the soul. Right in life everyone can practice the method of deliverance. ... If one waits until his/her death, what can he/she use to demonstrate whether he/she succeeds in the deliverance or not? If people must wait until their death to achieve spiritual deliverance, divine beings would not advice humans to engage in the Way, to teach the Way to this world*

---

[22] Đức Quan Âm Bồ Tát; Thánh thất Bình Hòa, Ngọ thời, the eighth day of the fourth month of Canh Tuất year (May 12, 1970).

so that everyone becomes perfectly virtuous and be able to enjoy the paradise right on Earth. While being alive, if one cannot renovate his/her thoughts to align with those of virtuous beings, regardless of the hundred or thousand times of death, he/she remains mortal and keeps transmigrating accordingly with his/her karmic rhythm. [23]

So far, we have only discussed cultivating and salvaging oneself. To save other people is a much more challenging task, because if he/she cannot demonstrate to other people any real evidence of his/her spiritual attainment and instead, he/she just uses speculative reasoning, he/she could hardly convince anyone to believe in him/her.

Đức Quan Âm Bồ Tát taught:

Brothers and sisters! In this physical world people usually follow, listen to, and act accordingly to what they hear, see, touch, or feel. For them, the moral norms are merely some vague and abstract words. It would be very difficult to apply the moral norms to make them awakened, if there is no strong and logical discussion to demonstrate the fact, which is a challenging task for the religious leaders. Because humans are born in this world, they grow up in this world, and at death their bodies also decompose in this world. If throughout the lifetime from birth to death, a person's speech and deed do not demonstrate any qualities of a virtuous being to inspire other people toward goodness, whether he/she could become immortal or buddha cannot

---

[23] Đức Vạn Hạnh Thiền Sư; Minh Lý Thánh Hội, Tuất thời, the eighth day of the fourth month of Canh Tuất year (May 12, 1970).

guarantee for such speculative reasoning of the religious leader.[24]

How to resolve this challenging issue? Đức Quan Âm Bồ Tát taught a basic solution: Frequently review your inner. At least once per day, everyone should reflect on his/her inner, applying justice and impartiality to judge him/herself. He/she should evaluate if his/her thoughts, speech, and deeds during that day are against or in accord with the moral norms. When getting used to this habit, everyone should implement it more frequently—not every day, but every hour, every minute—to control his/her own body, to adjust his/her own actions in every instant of his/her life.[25]

Divine beings name this method the <u>Egoless Review</u>.

Review in this context means *self-review* or *self-judgement* against the past events to gradually *self-control, self-educate, self-guide* in the coming events or in the future.

Egoless in this context means to remove from the inner the profane ego, the opaque self of ignorance.

Hence, *egoless review* means to get rid of the ego to self-review, self-control, self-educate.

Performing *egoless review* always requires one's own efforts to clear up his//her heart from the inside and make his/her virtues and talents shine up to the outside.

---

[24] Đức Quan Âm Bồ Tát; Minh Lý Thánh Hội, Tuất thời, the 16th day of the sixth month of Canh Tuất year (July 18, 1970).

[25] Đức Quan Âm Bồ Tát; Minh Lý Thánh Hội, Tuất thời, the 16th day of the sixth month of Canh Tuất year (July 18, 1970).

Whoever can self-enlighten his/her heart, conduct, virtue, and talent is the one who knows how to implement the principle *Make of yourself a light* to achieve the spiritual deliverance.

We are discussing how to demonstrate to humans the convincing outcomes of the deliverance. A light made of one's self not only illuminates the way for that person, but also guides other people living with him/her, surrounding him/her, or having some relationship with him /her.

Đức Quan Âm Bồ Tát says the following of such person:

Though living in this world, being a citizen like all other citizens, but his/her insight, thoughts, speech are perfectly standard, virtuous, demonstrating, and modelling, whereas his/her deeds are entirely beneficial to other people. As such, although he/she has not freed from the physical body, his/her heart is already delivered from the material world, because his/her thoughts, deeds, and speech are perfectly within the norms of goodness, beauty, and benevolence comparable to those of buddhas and immortals. Wouldn't such person be regarded and loved as a superman?[26]

Someone might counterargue by asking why the cultivator should bother him/herself with the proof finding. According to this argument, the cultivator should know his/her success discreetly with no need to demonstrate it to other people, and therefore no need to convince or prove to anyone else whether the deliverance leads to any outcomes.

---

[26] Đức Quan Âm Bồ Tát; Minh Lý Thánh Hội, Tuất thời, the 16th day of the sixth month of Canh Tuất year (July 18, 1970).

With respect to this counterargument, there are two points to be clarified.

- First, the demonstration of the deliverance outcomes is primarily for self-evidence; by proving it objectively, one would not deceive oneself with unrealistic assumptions.

- Second, when and only when the result is evidenced by other people, the cultivator can guide and save them.

Let's get into the details of each of these two points.

The first point is to demonstrate one's deliverance outcomes to oneself.

Quite a few people devote themselves in cultivation only to *expect to become immortal or buddha,*[27] or in other words, *to deliver from all worldly matter, including the eating, drinking, and the living in this world, to attain some kinds of happier, longer-lasting paradise or nirvana.*[28]

Then they pretend for themselves the unreal qualities that they consider as the deliverance outcomes; for example, the quality of *always knowing in advance the divine will,* or *hearing the quiet voice,* or *seeing strange spectacles while sitting in meditation,* or *always finding their lost money,* etc. …

Those qualities sound more like the expression of their own desires than the peace of a tranquil mind.

The Way (the Dao) is innate in every being and the Way is our life. Therefore, the attainment of the Way, if that

---

[27] Đức Vạn Hạnh Thiền Sư; Minh Lý Thánh Hội, Tuất thời, the eighth day of the fourth month of Canh Tuất year (May 12, 1970).

[28] Đức Quan Âm Bồ Tát; Thánh thất Bình Hòa, Ngọ thời, the eighth day of the fourth month of Canh Tuất year (May 12, 1970).

is true, should be very realistic and expressed in every thought, speech, and deed in the cultivator's daily life.

The reason people wish to evade reality to seek the unreal worlds in their imagination is merely because they do not attain the Way of reality mentioned in the following holy teaching: *because they no longer see the Way, they look for it farther to maintain their hope.*[29]

In Francis Bacon's language,[30] we can say that such cultivators not only fail the deliverance but also doom the triple slavery: slavery to desire, slavery to imagination, and slavery to mental hunger.

In the first slavery, they let their desires deceive them, making them believe that they achieve the objectives of the spiritual cultivation.

In the second slavery, their imagination let them enjoy the cake image (not the real cake!).

Then in the third slavery, though having known the true Dharma of the Great Way, they do not absorb it:

> *Like a group of people dying of thirst alongside the water stream, a group of people dying of hunger on the granary, a herd of sheep being weary on the green lawn, and the cultivators being dry and barren on the stream of teaching, fallen at the port of awakening.*[31]

---

[29] Đức Quan Âm Bồ Tát; Thánh thất Bình Hòa, Ngọ thời, the eighth day of the fourth month of Canh Tuất year (May 12, 1970).

[30] William James Durant, *The Story of Philosphy*, Vietnamese translated version *Câu chuyện Triết học*, Đà Nẵng Publisher, 2000, page 123.

[31] Đức Giáo Tông Vô Vi Đại Đạo; Ngọc Chiếu Đàn, Ngọ thời, the fifth day of the first month of Ất Tỵ year (Feb. 06, 1965).

To avoid those scenarios, the cultivator should prove objectively to him/herself about how far he/she is on the way to spiritual deliverance.

The second point is to demonstrate the deliverance outcomes to humans. Only with these proofs, people can believe that the salvation grace of the Great Way is an actual verity and not an unreal legend.

Cao Dai disciples cannot cultivate only for themselves, but also for the entirety of mankind—if not for all living beings. That is a duty, not an option of their preference. Đức Lý Giáo Tông insisted the following:

Caodaists must be the model, the boat, the bridge to deliver mankind from the port of ignorance to that of awakening, the transceiver of kinetic energy to promote the doctrinal union, and the nature of Creation to incorporate loving-kindness in the entire mankind.[32]

Every Cao Dai disciple should self-cultivate until becoming a flawless example to humans, an *example to inspire mankind to goodness, example to wake ignoring people.*[33]

Once the excellent models emerge more and more numerously in the society, the world itself will also change:

Brothers and sisters, you should consider the cultivation, the religious activities, and the deliverance per se. You should have such an action plan right in this world to make the name for the

---

[32] Đức Giáo Tông Vô Vi Đại Đạo; Ngọc Minh Đài, Tuất thời, the 15th day of the seventh month of Canh Tuất year (Aug. 16, 1970).

[33] Đức Vô Cực Từ Tôn; Ngọc Minh Đài,Tuất thời, the 15th day of the fourth month of Mậu Thân year (May 11, 1968).

Way. Only when the name is made, people in this world would respect and follow you in the self-cultivation and become virtuous. If one person imitates you to self-cultivate and becomes virtuous, dozens of others do so, hundreds, thousands, millions of people do so, then this world would no longer be a full ocean of grieves; instead, it is the paradise on Earth.[34]

Therefore, to save the world, Caodaists should become exemplary to humans; the key of being an example is to demonstrate it, not by merely reasoning but by actual success in the spiritual way of deliverance.

To demonstrate it we need to show real evidences. What should we look for within ourselves as proofs of deliverance?

4. PROOFS OF DELIVERANCE: HUMAN FRATERNITY AND UNIVERSAL HARMONY

The degree of deliverance that a cultivator achieves should be gauged through the extent of harmony in his/her life. The level of forming and developing a harmonious community and/or union is the most important evidence of a Caodaist's degree of deliverance.

In Bính Dần year 1926, at Gò Kén pagoda, right within the period of the Inauguration Ceremony of Caodaism, God affirmed: *I, your Master, come to establish*

---

[34] Đức Quan Âm Bồ Tát; Minh Lý Thánh Hội, Tuất thời, the 16th day of the sixth month of Canh Tuất year (July 18, 1970).

the Third Universal Salvation, employing only one word: Harmony.[35]

Failing to achieve harmony, the Caodaists could never accomplish their mission. Therefore, no matter how long a Caodaist has practiced the deliverance cultivation, and how high standing he/she has promoted in the method of heart, if he/she cannot fraternize with other people, he/she has no evidence to prove to him/herself (as well as to all human beings), or to make everyone believe that he/she can attain enlightenment in this current lifetime.

The Third Universal Salvation has its goal: *harmony in temporal way, deliverance in spiritual way.* This goal has been assigned to each individual Caodaist in the form of an order: *cultivate the deliverance and live in harmony.* This is not as an option of preference, as in either cultivating the deliverance or living in harmony, but a necessity to do both.

And both the deliverance and harmony must be successfully implemented right within oneself, right in this current life. Moreover, one is the condition for the other: To succeed in the cultivation of deliverance, one must learn to live in harmony. And vice versa: to succeed in the life of harmony, one must wilfully cultivate the way of deliverance. Only with such combination one could make of his/her being a light. Otherwise, the Caodaist pioneers would not insist on those stepping in the great vehicle[36] of spiritual deliverance as follows:

---

[35] Đức Ngọc Hoàng Thượng Đế; Từ Lâm Tự (Chùa Gò Kén), the 14th day of the first month of Đinh Mão year (Feb.13, 1927); Thánh Ngôn Hiệp Tuyển, Q.1.

[36] Translator's note: In Buddhism, the essence of the great vehicle or Mahanaya Buddhism is the conception of compassion for all living

Younger brothers, once getting into the doorstep of the great vehicle, you should self-enlighten your spark of light to break up all the darkness filled with errors and partition. Only by doing so, your inner can harmonize, mystically identifying to the creator, and your wisdom reveals to propagate the Dharma, saving mankind in this difficult time.[37]

The most important creatures that each Caodaist cultivator must harmonize with are the people around him, and not the immortals and buddhas already acceded to the heaven.

Whoever is not successful in self-deliverance cannot fraternize with other people on any level, and therefore, cannot live harmoniously in any community.

On the other hand, those who cannot fraternize with other people do not know how to establish a harmonious life with the communities he is living in; therefore, it is uncertain whether he could free himself from the transmigration cycle.

So, once decisively stepping in the spiritual way of deliverance, the cultivator must fraternize with other people if he/she wants to guarantee for his/her success, precisely what Divine Mother taught:

Children! The Way is not outside yourself, where the Dharma is the means. You understand the Way, practice the Way, then you can reveal the Dharma.

---

beings; it emphasizes the universalism and altruism, developing wisdom and the perfect transformation of all living in the future state.

[37] Chư Tiền Khai Đại Đạo; Cơ Quan Phổ Thông Giáo Lý, Tuất thời, the 15th day of the 10th month of Kỷ Mùi year (Dec. 04, 1979).

Once the Dharma is revealed, indeed you gain the power to help and guide humans.

Alas, children! If you cultivate but cannot evade the cycle of delusion and clinging, sooner or later you would fall into the ignorance. If you want to fully awaken to penetrate the mystic meaning of the Dharma of the Way, never should you forget the following treasures: harmony, humbleness, loving-kindness, tolerance, patience, perseverance, and sacrifice of all your personal belongings.

With these, you harmonize with the circumstances and people, and naturally you harmonize with the celestial law. With these, you will see neither the nonself or the self, neither the discipline or the demand. Without self and nonself, without discipline and demand, you implement correctly the moral norms, as well as the true Dharma of the Great Way.[38]

5. A LIFE OF CULTIVATION OF DELIVERANCE CAN ONLY BE SUCCESSFUL BASED ON A LIFE IN HARMONY

Almost all the key points on the topic of deliverance in the doctrine of the Great Way are tactfully summarized by Đức Quan Âm Bồ Tát in the following twelve verses:

Liberate means untie past karma,

Liberate means clear up wrongdoings.

Liberate from karmic debts with proactivity,

---

[38] Đức Vô Cực Từ Tôn; Vĩnh Nguyên Tự, Tuất thời, the 11th day of the 11th month of Bính Thìn year (Dec. 31, 1976).

Liberate from karmic links with willpower.

Liberate from the delusion of the sensible,

Liberate from the self-nonself differentiation,

Liberate from sufferings with self-cultivation,

Liberate to escape from the worldly net.

Free means nothing else than escape,

Free from disturbances to see the marvel.

Free does not mean denying secular duties,

Free means avoiding all wrongdoings.[39]

To "free," one should "liberate" first, i.e., untie him/herself, breaking up all his/her shackles. Here are the four keys to success, but all of them essentially are the life style of fraternity and harmony right in this dusty world of karma:

Liberate from karmic debts with proactivity,

Liberate from karmic links with willpower.

Liberate from the delusion of the sensible,

Liberate from the self-nonself differentiation.

Let's analyze each individual key: How is the key used to unblock the way to self-deliverance?

Fortunately, the answers for such questions could be readily found in the teaching of the Great Way.

How does one *liberate from karmic debts with proactivity?*

---

[39] Đức Quan Âm Bồ Tát; Thánh thất Bình Hòa, Ngọ thời, the eighth day of the fourth month of Canh Tuất year (May 12, 1970).

Few people can grasp the deliverance meaning from the word *proactivity*. The Jewish psychiatrist Viktor Frankl (1905-1997) experienced it during his years of imprisonment in the Nazi concentration camps. In the days facing his death, he discovered the meaning of proactivity in his efforts to remain alive. That meaning is simple. A proactive person takes responsibility and initiative of all his activities, including his thoughts, speech, and deeds. Thanks to this experience his inner was enlightened, allowing him to win over the violent power of the outside.

Studying that meaning, Stephen R. Covey (1932-2012) perceived this: Those who are not proactive usually live with *concern*. They are always concerned about other people's weaknesses, about the issues of the outside, about the factors that they cannot control; they use those concerns to blame and condemn other people and circumstances, as well as to advocate their own defects. On the other hand, proactive people do not live with *concern* and concentrate all their efforts to forge the *influence* of their inner to impact on the outside. Thanks to this, they take control of their circumstances.[40]

Therefore, the proactivity itself is a deliverance behavior of thought. This behavior helps us reach the first level of deliverance right in this world.

Đức Quan Âm Bồ Tát taught that *Deliverance from the stagnancy of selfish soul is to actively service and guide humans in this world.*[41]

---

[40] Stephen R. Covey, *The Seven Habits of Highly Effective People*, Vietnamese translated version *Bảy Thói Quen Của Những Người Thành Đạt* by Nguyễn Văn Cừ, Thống Kê Publisher, 1996, page 85.

[41] Đức Quan Âm Bồ Tát; Thánh thất Bình Hòa, Ngọ thời, the eighth day of the fourth month of Canh Tuất year (May 12, 1970).

To deliver from the somber of the self, the stagnancy of the selfishness, one must service mankind. This is the basic level of deliverance. But even at this level of the small vehicle,[42] Cao Dai disciples must perform work of merit to service others. Servicing here does not mean to exchange his/her work to gain hidden merit for him/herself, but to fulfill one of his/her duties in the Human Way. While having progressed several steps in this level, he/she should guide and save other people and cannot postpone this task until he/she becomes immortal or buddha. To *guide and save people* is the focus of the grand vehicle and belongs to the mission of the grand vehicle in the Great Way. Then this level of deliverance, although basic, seems not at all a low bar; instead, it is the foundation for all the three stages of the nine initiations in the Great Way.

How does one *liberate from karmic links with willpower?*

What are the karmic links that imprison us? They are the four dungeons *greed, anger, ignorance, and desire* that the new method of the Great Way teaches us how to evade:

> *Escape from the four dungeons,*
>
> *Greed, anger, ignorance, and desire that blind all the four sides.*[43]

But what is the origin of those dungeons? Since the creation of Heaven and Earth, the Creator never creates

---

[42] Translator's note: The small vehicle or Hylayana Buddhism focuses on personal salvation. It seeks the destruction of body and mind to be reborn in nirvana.

[43] Đức Đông Phương Chưởng Quản; Cơ Quan Phổ Thông Giáo Lý, Tuất thời, the fourth day of the sixth month of Tân Dậu year (July 05, 1981).

them. Then who did? It is each individual who built those dungeons for oneself. Đức Quan Âm Bồ Tát taught:

People created the four dungeons,

Once being trapped they find no way to exit;

Though invisible to corporal eyes,

The dungeons are infinitely high and unfathomably deep.[44]

Here is the most grimly humoured puzzle for every human: We built the dungeons to imprison ourselves, and created the shackles to chain ourselves. Such creation generated the most frightening fetter systems in this world. They are so horrible that Đức Chơn Thường Đạo Sĩ, after passing away and successfully returning to the immortal realm, recalled his transmigrated lives in those dungeons and pitifully lamented:

There, it is known as the four dungeons,

Having the entrance but no exit,

Without the sword of wisdom,

Hardly can the ignorance curtain be unveiled.[45]

What is the sword of wisdom? It is the definitiveness in breaking up with the deluded heart and preserving the true heart. Đức Quan Âm Bồ Tát taught:

Indeed, the definitiveness between delusion and truth is so extraordinary in this world. To quickly

---

[44] Đức Quan Âm Bồ Tát; Hườn Cung Đàn, Tý thời, the eighth day of the fourht month of Ất Tỵ year (May 07, 1965).

[45] Đức Chơn Thường Đạo Sĩ; Minh Lý Thánh Hội, Hợi thời, the 14th day of the seventh month of Canh Tuất year (Aug. 15, 1970).

progress on the cultivation way, besides implementing the mottos readily found in the doctrine, you should maintain your original nature perfectly good and aesthetic, also avoid the cases of reciting prayers and bowing to Buddha at one time, alms offering at another time, yet being jealous of other people, greedy and selfish at the other time. That is to maintain your cultivation stature at full balance.[46]

This holy recommendation gives us a practical formula to quit the deluded heart by looking back into the inner, egolessly reviewing it, and weeding out all greed, anger, ignorance, and desire. Except for the enlightened beings who are still in this world, the rest—all of us —has a similar inner profile of the "self" . Vividly displayed in that "self" profile are greed, anger, ignorance, and desire. Greed and desire are easily recognized, but anger and ignorance seem harder to observe.

Đức Quan Âm taught us that to recognize the anger nature of the "self", one should self-monitor to find the level at which the "self" is jealous of other people. This jealousy is the most typical representative for the *anger* nature, because the essence of anger is the dissension, looking for the differences between oneself and others.

How about the *ignorance* nature? It is nowhere farther; its agency is the selfishness, because the essence of ignorance is the delusion, the love of oneself.

It turns out that we are guilty of *living among the evils of impermanence but not knowing it.* Furthermore, *those evils are mingling in the material life, in the cognitive*

---

[46] Đức Quan Âm Bồ Tát; Thánh thất Bình Hòa, Ngọ thời, the eighth day of the fourth month of Canh Tuất year (May 12, 1970).

heart, in the karma-accumulating heart. They provoke all kinds of anger, ignorance, dispute, selfishness.... [47]

Therefore, to escape from the karmic cycle and from the imprisonment of ignorance that we have continuously built up, we can only rely upon ourselves, and no divine beings can do this for us.

Đức Bảo Pháp Chơn Quân Huỳnh Chơn taught us as follows: *It is necessary to definitively leave the evils of impermanence—seeing impermanence, hearing impermanence, speech impermanence—for the inner master to become steady and unhindered.* [48]

How does one *liberate from the delusion of the sensible*?

To liberate from the delusion, one should really understand where and how he/she is deluded. Moreover, he/she should intermingle with the mass to find whether he/she is deluded or not. Anyone who lives in isolation can assert that he/she is always awakened, simply because he/she does not have a chance to experience the full clashes and challenges posed by human fellows in this world.

Speaking of the *sensible*—which are *sound* and *form*—is speaking of the matter that the ears can hear, the eyes can see by contacting with the outside. And speaking of *thought* is speaking of the matter that the mind contemplates and those being assumed that we understand or know from such contacts.

---

[47] Đức Bảo Pháp Huỳnh Chơn; Minh Đức Tu Viện, Hợi thời, the 27th day of the first month of Tân Dậu year (March 03, 1981).

[48] Đức Bảo Pháp Huỳnh Chơn; Minh Đức Tu Viện, Hợi thời, the 27th day of the first month of Tân Dậu year (March 03, 1981).

There is a scary paradox but also a valuable gift for those who can think arbitrarily: *Our thought and knowledge are not right if they are based on the sensible, and neither are they right if they are not based on the sensible.*

Philosophers discovered this paradox a long time ago. According to the empiricists, thought becomes futile if not based on the sensible. On the other hand, the rationalists stated that if thought is based on the sensible, it is deceived by the sensible.

This dilemma of thought—as stated in the teaching of the Way from past to present—is the delusion of thought. The reason human thought is deluded by the sounds and forms in this world is because humans are still ego-clinging when interacting with other people.

Đức Quan Âm Bồ Tát taught the following:

As long as he/she still clings to his/her ego, he/she remains in delusion, greed, anger, and ignorance. Remaining in delusion, greed, anger, and ignorance means remaining in the endless cycle of cause and effect.[49]

How does one liberate thought from this dilemma, or in other words, how does one *liberate oneself from the delusion of the sensible?*

Everyone should cure oneself from one's ego-clinging. If the seeing, hearing, knowing are absolutely egoless, preserve them; on the other hand, if they are tinged with the self, soberly discard them.

Đức Quan Âm Bồ Tát taught this:

---

[49] Đức Quan Âm Bồ Tát; Cơ Quan Phổ Thông Giáo Lý, Tuất thời, the 15th day of the seventh month of Đinh Tỵ (Aug. 29, 1977).

If all the seeing, hearing, knowing in common sense are discarded, the radiant spirit would reveal, lighting all the hindrances in the world to break up the darkness of the six perceptions so that all beings can return to the awakening shore.[50]

How does one *liberate from the self-nonself differentiation?*

To dissipate the emotions originated from the self, Đức Vạn Hạnh Thiền Sư taught us a simple but effective method:

Any time you want to criticize someone's fault, reflect on yourself whether you committed that fault in the past; if yes, forgive him. Any time you feel upset at someone, ask your own conscience whether you need to be comforted with affectionate words in a constructive attitude; if yes, forgive him and apply those solutions to help him. Keep practicing and straining yourself all the time. In every situation, forge your heart to be compassionate for other people. In the long run, your heart is naturally filled with infinite love, nobleness and calmness. These qualities manifest as the respectful and sympathetic traits on your face.[51]

Therefore, seeking the answers for the implementation of the keys to self-liberate and self-unleash from all fetters, we can draw a formula of success for those

---

[50] Đức Quan Âm Bồ Tát; Cơ Quan Phổ Thông Giáo Lý, Tuất thời, the 15th day of the seventh month of Đinh Ty year (Aug. 29, 1977).

[51] Đức Vạn Hạnh Thiền Sư; Minh Lý Thánh Hội, Tuất thời, the eighth day of the fourth month of Canh Tuất year (May 12, 1970).

Caodaists who know how to live and cultivate effectively. This formula is as follows:

- Cultivate the spiritual deliverance by living in harmony.
- Live in harmony by cultivating the spiritual deliverance.

Applying this formula to the expedition of the spiritual deliverance, a life of self-cultivation can only succeed if based on a life of harmony. Utilizing your own fraternity and harmony to **egolessly review** your results in the cultivation of deliverance is to *Make of yourself a light* toward the ultimate goal of the Great Way for the Third Universal Salvation.

6. CONCLUDING NOTES

The genuine results of the deliverance always lie in the self-forging of our inner, and not in scriptures or in divine blessing. Therefore, on the spiritual way of deliverance, you should *rely upon yourself, upon the true Dharma, do not depend upon anything else.* Sakyamuni Buddha stated, *After I leave the world, whoever can learn and cultivate exactly that way is the excellent cultivator.*

Quite a few Caodaists are proud of their religion merely because it bears the name Great Way for the Third Universal Salvation. Yet, Đức Đông Phương Chưởng Quản mercifully woke them up with a warning:

The name Great Way for the Third Universal Salvation is only symbolized in the form of Cao Dai Church, its dignitaries and personnel; yet, its content has nothing comparable to the Immortal stature. That is the very serious shortcoming in the great mission of this selected people.[52]

In the Great Way for the Third Universal Salvation, God lets his disciples make of themselves a light. Do not consider it as something worth worrying; instead, call it a training. Only with such training Cao Dai disciples can attain enlightenment in this current life to serve examples for mankind in both harmony in the temporal way and deliverance in the spiritual way.

If Caodaism cannot provide such disciples, there is no hope for convincing mankind that Cao Dai way is really the Great Way. By merely preaching the holy teaching to the world, Caodaism cannot be the Great Way in the cognition of mankind. No matter how crucial this preaching is, it is the enlightened people that are in demand.

Therefore, having received the new method of the Great Way, regardless of which level in the three stages of the nine initiations, Cao Dai disciples must dutifully and successfully implement what divine beings call *the purely true Dharma of the Way, the spiritual attainment of deliverance.*

God's work on this Third Universal Salvation creates the right combination of Heaven and Earth for everyone who is determined to make of himself a light on the way to deliverance:

Cultivate and get the ten-fold interest,

---

[52] Đức Đông Phương Chưởng Quản, Bác Nhã Tịnh Đường, the 24th day of the fourth month of Quý Sửu year (May 26, 1973).

In the heavenly bank God Father saves for you.[53]

So, right here and right now, this is the greatest opportunity for anyone who wants to enrich his spiritual account so as to be able to share it with all creatures.

Speech delivered at
The Organization for Preaching the Doctrine of the Great Way
on May 9, 2009 (the 15th day of the fourth month of Kỷ Sửu
year)

---

[53] Đức Quan Âm Bồ Tát, Giáo Hội Tiên Thiên Minh Đức, the 20th day of the ninth month of Đinh Mùi year (Oct. 23, 1967)

HOW TO INAUGURATE THE GREAT WAY

Given the chance to witness the Inauguration of the Great Way in Bính Dần year (1926), the majority of mankind might have thought it was the publication of a new religion. Quite a few Cao Dai followers also believed it was the proclamation of Caodaism.

But why does everyone in this religion, divine beings as well as human beings, call this special day the Inauguration of the Great Way (or in short, the Inauguration of the Way), instead of the Inauguration of Caodaism?

Đức Vạn Hạnh Thiền Sư taught :

People regard it as Cao Dai religion,

Unaware of it as the Great Way in propagation [54]

Speaking of Caodaism is referring to a new religion founded in Vietnam. But mentioning the Great Way, Đức Đông Phương Lão Tổ taught:

The Great Way is not bound to time. It is not anterior nor posterior; neither is it old or new; the Great Way is merely the immutable intrinsic essence. [55]

---

[54] Đức Vạn Hạnh Thiền Sư; Trúc Lâm Thánh Đức Thiền Điện, Tuất thời, the seventh day of the third month of Giáp Dần year (March 30, 1974).

[55] Đức Đông Phương Chưởng Quản; Cơ Quan Phổ Thông Giáo Lý, Tuất thời, the 15th day of the ninth month of Giáp Dần year (Oct. 29, 1974).

The Great Way's inauguration on the 15th day of the tenth lunar month is both Cao Dai religion and the immutable essence that surpasses Cao Dai religion, extending beyond all historical settings, and having the stature of the entire mankind.

That original essence is readily innate in every human heart and intrinsic in life; yet, people have long forgotten it.

Đức Vân Hương Thánh Mẫu taught:

God opens the Way to unveil the ignorant curtain that covers up the intrinsic essence in humans, to free the precious treasure that is deeply buried in human defective bodies and anxiously moaning of the worldly illusions.[56]

Inaugurating the Way means *removing the ignorant veil* that buries the human nature and conceals the God nature.

But inaugurating the Way within each individual is still insufficient, as the Way must also be radiated throughout the world, i.e., the flame of humaneness should be lit up brightly in all social classes.

That is the significance of the Inauguration of the Great Way. Nevertheless, grasping the meaning is one thing, but implementing it is another thing.

That is why the most important event delineated in the grand ceremony on the 15th day of the tenth month of Bính Dần year (1926) at Gò Kén Pagoda was God's

---

[56] Đức Vân Hương Thánh Mẫu; Chơn Lý Đàn, Tuất thời, the first day of the leap fourth month of Giáp Dần year (May 22, 1974).

message on how to implement the meaning of the Inauguration of the Great Way.

To accomplish the Inauguration of the Great Way, it is inadequate to merely organize a grand ceremony; instead, it requires the real people of the Great Way who can withstand all harsh challenges in life while maintaining their mighty willpower to radiate the light of humaneness all over the world.

To be entrusted with such a tremendous mission, those people should be selected in open view of the entirety of mankind and the heaven-earth. And this selection occurred through a grand trial at midnight of the 15th day of the tenth month of Bính Dần year (1926).

Over fifty years after that event, Đức Giáo Tông Vô Vi Đại Đạo explained it as follows:

> *In the first anniversary of the Inauguration of the Great Way, God established a grand assessment to select the candidates for the propagation of the Great Way. The first disciples, who were determined to attain spiritual deliverance, willfully overcame all harsh challenges. God entrusted them with the mission of mystic power for the Third Universal Salvation on this turbulent country.*[57]

The Inauguration of the Great Way is an ideological symbol for a more important issue, which is that Caodaist disciples should successfully enlighten the Great Way in their own heart, and Caodaist leaders should successfully enlighten the Great Way in every community of mankind.

---

[57] Đức Giáo Tông Đại Đạo Tam Kỳ Phổ Độ; CQ Phổ Thông Giáo Lý, Hợi thời, the 15th day of the tenth month of Mậu Ngọ year (Nov. 15, 1978).

Caodaist Predecessors reminded us of the following:

Brothers and sisters! The fact that God came to inaugurate the Great Way was an extraordinary event, but the propagation of the Great Way to save all beings would also be another extraordinary reality.[58]

If we, Cao Dai disciples, fail to make the significance of the Inauguration of the Great Way a reality, no matter how many anniversaries of this event have passed—eighty years, ninety years, or a hundred years— still the Great Way has not yet been meaningfully inaugurated for the Viet people and all of mankind.

In Bính Dần year 1986, on the 60th anniversary of the Inauguration of the Great Way, Đức Lý Giáo Tông expressed his sentiments as follows:

Sisters! Do you recall God's message on Bính Dần year 1926? One day late for the Way being preached to mankind is another detrimental day people have to bear. This message was taught sixty years ago but it is still valid and significant. On the anniversary of the Inauguration of the Great Way, I feel more burdened with this responsibility....[59]

The Inauguration of the Great Way comes again this year. In the sincere and warm atmosphere of the festival, all children of God, regardless of their diverse churches or branches, reserve a special affection for this grand festival.

---

[58] Chư Tiền Khai Đại Đạo Tam Kỳ Phổ Độ; CQ Phổ Thông Giáo Lý, Tuất thời, the 14th day of the second month of Giáp Dần year (March 07, 1974).

[59] Đức Giáo Tông Vô Vi Đại Đạo; Cơ Quan Phổ Thông Giáo Lý, the 15th day of the tenth month of Bính Dần year (Nov. 16, 1986).

When their hearts unify into such a common spirit, this is the once-in-a-year chance to *restore the mighty and inspiring lifeline for the Great Way.*[60]

To succeed in making such an event a reality, let us kindle the light brightly. In every thought and speech, in every religious activity, let us spark up our own lights. Let us then spread the inspiration and transfer the light to other people to ignite many more lights.

Do not inadvertently put out any light. Let us relay each other, spark each other's light, save each other's light, to brighten up the Way and radiate the awareness of the mission of the selected people.[61]

If God empowers us with an energetic workforce comprising talented and virtuous individuals, but they do not inspire and relay each other, they would quickly become isolated, scattered, and lackluster collectives. As such, the only reality is that each individual would independently self-cultivate and never could the propagation of the Great Way be widespread, let alone become the national religion of Vietnam—or *a purely true entity of the Way for the universal salvation*[62] throughout the world.

Therefore, Cao Dai followers and leaders in this Third Universal Salvation should successfully spark up their own light to gather people, unify human hearts, and

---

[60] Chư Tiền Khai Đại Đạo Tam Kỳ Phổ Độ; Cơ Quan Phổ Thông Giáo Lý Đại Đạo,Tuất thời, the 14th day of the second month of Giáp Dần year (March 07, 1974).

[61] Translator's note: "The selected people" is the term used by divine beings to indicate the Vietnamese people based on the fact that God founded the Great Way for the Third Universal Salvation in Vietnam.

[62] Cơ Quan Phổ Thông Giáo Lý, *Thánh Giáo Sưu Tập Năm Mậu Thân - Kỳ Dậu (1968-1969)*. Hà Nội: Nxb Tôn Giáo 2009, page. 110.

strengthen human resources. Any collectives whose enthusiasm is nurtured by such a brilliant light would be always ready to self-sacrifice for the ideal of the Great Way.

Only when such outlook becomes reality, can we successfully inaugurate the Great Way.

On the Anniversary of
The Inauguration of the Great Way
Kỷ Sửu year (2009)

THE SPRING IN HUMAN FRATERNITY

The Spring! Spring comes with all eagerness,

What is the spring that all beings await?

Spring is back when people enjoy wine and poetry,

Exchanging wishes and having break time.[63]

Any time the spring arrives, people in this world welcome it with excitement. Yet, not many wonder what the spring is and why they welcome it. Rich or poor, every home greets the spring willingly, sincerely, passionately, and warmly. Then *what is the spring that all beings await*?

Understanding the essence of the spring, not only do we greet it but we can also make a spring that everyone longs for: *The spring in human fraternity.*

1. WHAT IS THE SPRING?

Spring is the scene at culmination of heaven-earth favor.[64]

Only with human fraternity, spring becomes the true spring.

Years and months fly past endlessly.

---

[63] Đức Giáo Tông Vô Vi Đại Đạo, Cơ Quan Phổ Thông Giáo Lý, the 29th day of the 12th month of Mậu Ngọ year (Jan. 27, 1979).

[64] Translator's note: It is translated from the Vietnamese idiom "thiên thời địa lợi."

Knowing the spring, you can enjoy the splendid spring climes.[65]

Human life consists of two parts: the exterior part is the interactions with the outside, while the interior one is the activities of the inner.

Regarding the exterior life, spring is merely one of the four seasons originated from the heaven-earth operation.

But as of the interior life, spring is an inner state originated from human harmony. Heaven-earth employs the spectacles to depict the spring look, but it is mankind that employs fraternity to create the spring spirit. Only when human fraternity incorporates the spring scene can the spring look gain its spirit, and the spring season exist in human sentiments.

Knowing it, on the occasion of Tết,[66] the Vietnamese usually create a warm atmosphere in the gatherings of family or community to nurture the harmony with their ancestors, to tighten the fraternity between people of the present, and to sympathize with each other in every wish for the future.

With thousands of Tết events in the Viet history, the Tết gathering has become a holy symbol of human fraternity in the internal perception of the Vietnamese.

There are families that can gather for only one day

---

[65] Đức Giáo Tông Vô Vi Đại Đạo, Cơ Quan Phổ Thông Giáo Lý, the 29th day of the 12th month of Mậu Ngọ year (Jan. 27, 1979).

[66] Translator's note : Tết is Vietnamese New Year's Day, which is the first day of a lunar calendar.

at the end of the year, the Lunar New Year's Eve, just for hastily cleaning up the house together, preparing the offerings to the ancestors together, and making traditional treats for the Tết festival together.

In such "together" activities, although everyone is unceasingly occupied and keeps lamenting about the endless list of tasks to be done, happiness always reveals itself on their faces as they recognize that these gatherings are extremely precious.

On the first or second day of the new year, they must separate from each other due to their businesses. For such families, the day filled with the most spring atmosphere is the lunar New Year's Eve, because it is the day of fraternity, even though they fraternize merely to do relentless hard work from dawn to midnight, transitioning into the new year.

In those days of Tết, if discord unfortunately happens and heats up into disputes between family members or in neighborhood, the Tết atmosphere seems completely lost despite the flying birds covering the sky and the apricot blossoms blooming in front of the house. No way can the spring look from the culmination of heaven-earth make up for the grief caused by human discord.

This truly Vietnamese experience helps us understand why Đức Giáo Tông Vô Vi Đại Đạo taught that *Only with human fraternity, spring becomes the true spring.*[67]

---

[67] Đức Giáo Tông Vô Vi Đại Đạo, Cơ Quan Phổ Thông Giáo Lý, the 29th day of the 12th month of Mậu Ngọ year (Jan. 27. 1979).

Essentially, spring is harmony and the springtime is the season of fraternity. Without fraternity, the spring must harvest its failure although the spectacles are still completed with all the culmination of heaven-earth favor for a spring season.

Then what do we greet while welcoming the spring?

Deep down inside the mind of the Viet people, welcoming the spring means greeting the atmosphere of fraternity. Some people find it through the brief moments of warm gatherings, while many others keep expecting it but never have a chance to experience it.

Regardless, the fact that everyone awaits the spring reflects their longing for the fraternal life in mankind, the fraternity that is not found only in a spring season or in a community but also in every space and time of life.

In the degenerate era, such longing expresses the helplessness of mankind toward the disunion of the current world. No one wants to live in a discordant society, whether it is a discordant family or a discordant geographical area comprising many nations. Yet, the entire world is plunging into extreme discord, and the entirety of mankind is facing the risk of self-destruction due to its craving for violence.

What a dreary winter in the history of mankind! Everywhere in the world, discord crushes fraternity and sparks the extermination, let alone the natural calamities and epidemics that occur endlessly. The spectacles of the spring season that everyone thrillingly awaits every year absolutely cannot fix the problems. Therefore, in the spring season at the opening of the Great Way, God lamented:

Alas! Spring goes, spring comes. The spring of

mankind is about to fade off, and the spring of heaven-earth and of spectacles may not be everlasting, either.[68]

Fortunately, God initiated the Third Universal Salvation to establish the foundation for the restoration of this world. He taught the following: *I, your Master, open the Third Universal Salvation to save you, children, and the entire mankind, like the spring coming to all creatures.*[69]

Through the Third Salvation, God bestows to mankind a mystic power to transform *winter into spring, profane into saint, chaos into order, war into peace, egocentrism into universal harmony,*[70] to establish the virtuous era.

The virtuous era is a spring season that Caodaists must create for the survival of mankind, to free humans from the winter of the degenerate era. As the true spring can only exist with human fraternity, Caodaists must successfully create fraternity anywhere they wish to bring the virtuous spring to.

Human fraternity is a concept employed in Cao Dai teaching to indicate a model of fraternal society established on the three standards: humaneness, peacefulness, and progress.

This fraternal society should be able to improve all

---

[68] The Holy See Tòa Thánh Tây Ninh, *Thánh Ngôn Hiệp Tuyển* (*The Collection of Holy Teachings*), Vol. 2, Séance on Feb. 10, 1929.

[69] Cao Dai God, Cơ Quan Phổ Thông Giáo Lý, the 30th day of the 12th month of Giáp Dần year (Feb.10, 1975).

[70] Đức Giáo Tông Vô Vi Đại Đạo, Thánh thất Nam Thành, the first day of the first month of Kỷ Dậu year (Feb. 17, 1969).

other societies by exemplifying its concrete outcomes, making other societies follow it to gradually become fraternal societies.

Đức Lê Văn Duyệt Đại Tiên taught the following:

To create the stance of human fraternity is to establish a model society that can improve all other societies based on the three standards: humaneness, peacefulness, and progress.[71]

With respect to the fraternity stance in the Great Way, the three standards—humaneness, peacefulness, and progress—are of equal importance; they complement each other to keep the society in balance. Efforts to achieve all three standards gradually move the society toward human fraternity. Therefore, these three standards are considered the three legs of the fraternity stance.

The spring in human fraternity is the virtuous spring that Caodaists altogether should establish, to demonstrate the preservation functionality of the restoration mechanism. But to establish the saintly age for all of mankind in the future, starting now, Caodaists should successfully bring the virtuous spring to their churches, or at least to the organization within those churches where they perform their religious duties. This is a great mission for Caodaists, not only as children of God but also as the Viet people.

To accomplish this mission Caodaists must successfully establish the three-legged stance: *humaneness, peacefulness*, and *progress*.

---

[71] Đức Lê Văn Duyệt Đại Tiên, Cơ Quan Phổ Thông Giáo Lý, the 15th day of the second month of Canh Tuất year (March 21, 1970).

2. THE HUMANE SPRING

In a true spring, everyone can feel the warmness of heart through the sacred affections brought by his/her community, making him/her feel as though he/she belongs within that community. These sacred affections are the fusion between loving-kindness, pride, collective spirit, and the wish to serve others. It is an innate affection that links individuals into society and forms the base for societal morality. Cao Dai teaching names it *humaneness*.

Đức Lê Đại Tiên taught to *Aim all activities at humaneness, at the sacred affection that God bestows to each person.*[72]

Humaneness is the human essence, i.e., the essence based on which we achieve in ourselves the noble values of a human being and live with these values as a true man.

In personal life, that essence is human nature. Promoting that essence through each person's daily activities would determine the level of *being human*, and therefore, the extent of *becoming true man* that he really achieves.[73]

---

[72] Đức Lê Văn Duyệt Đại Tiên, Cơ Quan Phổ Thông Giáo Lý, the 15th day of the second month of Canh Tuất year (March 21, 1970).

[73] In this context, the concept (*làm người) being human* is extracted from the topic Sứ Mạng Vi Nhân (The Mission of Being Human) in *Yếu Điểm Giáo Lý Đại Đạo* (*Essentials in the Doctrine of the Great Way*), Cơ Quan Phổ Thông Giáo Lý Đại Đạo, Tôn Giáo Publisher, Hà Nội 2008, page 181.

The concept (*nên người) becoming true man* is extracted from the verse *Nên ta, nên đạo, mới nên người (Becoming youself, becoming the Way, then becoming true man)*, Đức Giáo Tông Vô Vi Đại Đạo,

In societal life, humaneness is the spirit of selflessness, egolessness, sacrifice for the loving-kindness toward the community.[74]

The noble values such as *selflessness* (dispose of one's self), *egolessness* (not clinging to one's profane ego), *sacrifice* (willing to accept all disadvantages to oneself), or *loving-kindness toward other people* (willing to self-devote to the mass public) are called the humane values, because they reveal human nature too obviously to be confused with any other nature.

Humaneness serves the first leg for the stance of human fraternity. If loving-kindness toward other people is so extended that we can devote ourselves, dispose of our ego, and willingly accept all disadvantages to ourselves, then that loving-kindness is developed to the extreme. And reaching the extreme, such loving-kindness becomes human fraternity.

According to Đức Vân Hương Thánh Mẫu's holy teaching, fraternity can be understood in the following:

The culmination of loving-kindness, no more no less, no bias, no self nor nonself, no racial discrimination, no religious differentiation; it is just the utmost goal to bring happiness and peacefulness back to life in this world, which should be no longer

---

Cơ Quan Phổ Thông Giáo Lý, the 29th day of the 12th month of Mậu Ngọ year (Jan. 27. 1979).

[74] Cơ Quan Phổ Thông Giáo Lý Đại Đạo, *Yếu Điểm Giáo Lý Đại Đạo (Essentials in the Doctrine of the Great Way)*, page 222.

divided by race.[75]

Therefore, humaneness is the core of human fraternity. Whoever promotes the humane values in his societal life will also promote human nature in his own personal life. On the other hand, the more human nature is promoted in an individual life, the more humane values are built up in society. Succeeding in this mission, no matter how small or large the society, is to contribute in the establishment of the fraternal foundation for the whole world.

Every society cherishes and admires humane values. Nevertheless, if we observe the contemporary societies around us, rarely could we find those values in reality. It is because, according to the doctrine of the Great Way, modern societies share a common trait named *rootlessness* (having no root).

To fix this problem, Đức Đại Tiên Lê Văn Duyệt taught that *the fraternity stance should restore humane values, to guide people back to the life conforming to the true nature of mankind.*[76]

If any society, religious or non-religious, cannot thrive on the humane qualities (i.e., they are not based on the loving-kindness toward the mass public), all of its individual and collective contributions, even with goodwill, would result in extremely detrimental effects.

Đức Lê Đại Tiên taught that *any act of*

[75] Đức Vân Hương Thánh Mẫu, Thánh thất Nam Thành, the 10th day of the third month of Mậu Thân year (Apr. 07, 1968).

[76] Đức Lê Văn Duyệt Đại Tiên; Cơ Quan Phổ Thông Giáo Lý, the 15th day of the second month of Canh Tuất year (March 21, 1970).

understanding, implementing, servicing, and serving beyond humaneness would lead to the fiercest consequences for society.[77]

To find its rationale, let us examine the truths of human behaviors.

Every human being (as God created) comprises love in their intrinsic essence. However, those who cannot love other people automatically turn all their love toward themselves. It makes them love their profane egos passionately. They may give a little bit of such love to those that their egos need, for instance, to the individuals, the factions, or the social classes that help satisfy their desires.

Consequently, in a society lacking the loving-kindness toward its mass public, there are always the individuals, factions, and social classes whose topmost priority is their own selfishness. Such society would plunge further and further into the mire of partition and discord.

It is the issue that Đức Lê Đại Tiên addressed as *the fiercest consequences for society.*

Therefore, no one can become a useful individual in society if he/she has not yet become a humane person.

Only when disposing of his/her profane ego, a person can prioritize the community benefits over the individual ones, and sacrifice him/herself to serve the public. Thus, in the initial period of the Great Way, on the occasion of the spring of Kỷ Tỵ year (1929), God taught this:

---

[77] Đức Lê Văn Duyệt Đại Tiên; Cơ Quan Phổ Thông Giáo Lý, the 15th day of the second month of Canh Tuất year (March 21, 1970).

Children, if you accept sufferings caused by this world, bear tortures generated by its circumstances, content with your disadvantages in the path of fame and wealth; if you are willing to lose for others to win, to mourn for others to laugh, to work laboriously for a living; to maintain the pure and tranquil mind, to refuse ill-gotten gains, to be compassionate, to love others more than yourself, it means you are bathing your soul into purity so as to get back to your Master.[78]

Successfully implementing this holy teaching, all Caodaists would become humane people, promoting their sacrifice in bringing the humane spring to the Way and to the world, to their churches and to the entire mankind.

3. THE PEACEFUL SPRING

In the thrilling atmosphere of the New Year's Day, people usually wish each other a happy new year. Associated with satisfaction, happiness is always expected from every spring season. Therefore, the spring in human fraternity cannot miss the peacefulness.

Being the second leg of the fraternity stance, peacefulness must be practiced in daily life. Đức Lê Đại Tiên taught: *If [peacefulness] has not been achieved, the fraternity stance cannot be named true fraternity.*[79]

---

[78] *Thánh Ngôn Hiệp Tuyển (The Collection of Holy Teachings)* Vol. 2, Séance on Feb. 10, 1929.

[79] Đức Lê Đại Tiên, Cơ Quan Phổ Thông Giáo Lý, the 15th day of the second month of Canh Tuất year (March 21, 1970).

Peacefulness is the happiness of a tranquil inner. This happiness exists when one can master his heart, not letting the outside influence it or other forces impact it.

In the peaceful spring, we are happy not because of the spring sunlight, the spring breeze, the spring festival, or the spring entertainment, but because of our heart being the master of itself in all life circumstances. The self-master ability of the inner with respect to the outside scenarios and outside forces is called *equanimity*.

In Caodaism, God taught that *equanimity and peacefulness are the two factors your Master utilizes to cultivate the Way.*[80]

Therefore, maintaining equanimity of the inner is a precious valor that every disciple must practice.

Facing the impermanence of this world, one can hope to liberate him/herself from the profane ego only when his/her inner is tranquil and from there, he/she evades all other dominant factors in the world.

For anyone living in such a self-controlled life, his/her inner would be calm and peaceful, his/her look would be content and free. Those qualities express satisfaction of his/her own life. And this satisfaction itself is happiness.[81] The more tranquil the inner, the longer-lasting this happiness.

How does peacefulness relate to humaneness?

---

[80] *Thánh Ngôn Hiệp Tuyển (The Collection of Holy Teachings) Vol. 2.* Séance on March 03, 1927.

[81] Refer to *Happiness in Caodaist Conception*, pages 101 – 113.

Not being tied to the profane ego, peacefulness is an egoless happiness.

As one achieves peacefulness, his/her heart opens itself to spread that happiness to everyone around him/her and creates a natural peace.

On the other hand, if one does not experience this happiness in his/her inner, he/she would have no way to fraternize with others. This can be tested. Any time one feels grievous, he/she usually causes unreasonable trouble to other people; but when he/she is happy, he/she is easier to be in concord with everyone.

However, among the seven emotional states of the ego, there are:

- Two states being the grief themselves: anger and sorrow.

- Two other states containing part of the grief due to their own emotional nature: hate and fear.

- The remaining three states can be immediately transformed into grief if they are not completely satisfied: love, happiness, and joy.

Most happiness we experience every day is impermanent; they result in brief moments of concord followed by innumerable periods of discord.

Only the peacefulness, i.e., the happiness originated from the peace of mind or the quietude of heart, has sufficient power to create a lasting peace in every societal relationship.

But never would a peaceful person, though calm and content, be a coward, seeking comfort for him/herself and avoiding heavy responsibilities to the mass public.

Willing to take charge of establishing the fraternal life for mankind without losing the equanimity of one's inner, a peaceful person would never get involved in fame, wealth, title, and power. In fact, he/she considers them the sullying causes of human personality.

The greatest reward for the peaceful person is knowing that all his/her hard work is beneficial to mankind. Đức Giáo Tông Vô Vi Đại Đạo taught the following:

Alas! The Noble One[82] in the past had only coarse grain for food and bent arm for a pillow, but all around the months and years there was no instant he did not think about how to benefit mankind, to put the nation in order, and to pacify the world.

During the interminable period he dragged his feet to the east, west, south, and north lands, he underwent innumerable challenges and hardships; yet, his mind still persisted in establishing the doctrine when leaving this impermanent world.

Throughout such lifetime, never did he focus his mind in trivial details around him, because he did not like to pursue fame and wealth. Yet, he was not deprived of anything. The Law of Creation recompensed him and arranged for him to finally become a blessed crane[83] flying to the heaven and

---

[82] Translator's note: The Noble One in this context is Confucius, the Founder of Confucianism.

[83] Translator's note : Throughout Asia, the crane is a symbol of long life and immortality. The crane is associated with longevity, health, happiness, wisdom and good luck. The White Crane can fly to the

leaving the doctrine named The Noble Ones for the world to revere and admire.[84]

Through the examples of the saints in the past, peacefulness has a very strange characteristic. It enriches humans in literal as well as figurative meaning. Peaceful people feel both their physical and spiritual life is so fulfilled, not because they own any material property or spiritual power, but because they can control their needs and achieve self-satisfaction. That sensation of fullness encourages them to share it with other people. Therefore, they easily gain other people's empathy and thanks to that empathy other people also readily fraternize with them.

In contrast, through the facts in the current world, those who do not attain peacefulness always feel lacking wealth, fame, title, power, social position, other people's respect, their own happiness, etc. It is not because they do not have those matters, but because they are under the constant control of their unlimited desire and selfishness. This feeling of deprivation makes them become demanding of others. But with constant demands they induce antipathy in other people, because everyone in this world feels annoyed by those who constantly make requests of them. Through such antipathy, they create discord.

Therefore, peacefulness functions to re-orient human needs and wishes. On one hand, it helps humans

---

heavens and it is a Chinese symbol for "wisdom" and is sometimes called the "heavenly" or "blessed" crane. (Source: https://en.wikipedia.org/wiki/Crane_(bird)).

[84] Đức Giáo Tông Vô Vi Đại Đạo, Cơ Quan Phổ Thông Giáo Lý, the 15th day of the seventh month of Tân Hợi year (Sep. 04, 1971).

give up the tendency of demanding from others for self-satisfaction, i.e., give up the tendency to create discord. On the other hand, it encourages humans to make an effort to seek happiness for mankind, i.e., encourage the effort to create human fraternity. These two functions terminate all conflicts regarding the needs and wishes of each society.

Thus, regarding the spring of human fraternity, Đức Lê Đại Tiên taught, *Human fraternity not only creates the calmness and stability in mankind, but also needs to establish peacefulness in the living life of mankind.*[85]

4. THE PROGRESSIVE SPRING

Progress is the third leg of fraternity stance.

The first leg, *humaneness*, relates to virtue and loving-kindness. The second leg, *peacefulness*, relates to happiness, peace, and concord. These two factors, *humaneness and peacefulness*, are necessary yet still insufficient. Đức Lê Đại Tiên taught that *Virtue and loving-kindness, happiness and peacefulness, they are still insufficient for a societal being. The must-have factor in the fraternity stance is progress.*[86]

In the traditional Tết (the lunar New Year's day), Vietnamese people usually wear new clothes to welcome the spring. New clothes symbolize freshness in all aspects of life in the coming year. The fact that everyone wears new clothes at the beginning of a new year symbolizes the wish

---

[85] Đức Lê Văn Duyệt Đại Tiên; Cơ Quan Phổ Thông Giáo Lý, the 15th day of the second month of Canh Tuất year (March 21, 1970).

[86] Đức Lê Văn Duyệt Đại Tiên; Cơ Quan Phổ Thông Giáo Lý, the 15th day of the second month of Canh Tuất year (March 21, 1970).

that each individual self-renovates so as to renovate the whole society altogether. That action shows expectations for individual and community progress.

What is progress? Đức Lê Đại Tiên taught, *Progress is perfectionation through time.*[87]

Progress is the perfectionation through time in every facet of human condition[88] and spirituality. If the progress is only made in several facets of life, for instance in science or economy, leaving morality and spirituality behind, it is not really the true progress and sometimes may cause an imbalance that results in the overall societal depression.

The spring in human fraternity should bring to individuals and society the progress in full. To achieve the common goals of the present and future, all members in a collective must be able to coordinate with each other in conception and cooperate with each other in action.

But according to Đức Lê Đại Tiên, to achieve this capacity, *the progress must be always brought up in all activity credos.*[89]

Each progress of the collective enhances the individual's values, and each progress of the individual

---

[87] Đức Lê Văn Duyệt Đại Tiên; Cơ Quan Phổ Thông Giáo Lý, the 15th day of the second month of Canh Tuất year (March 21, 1970).

[88] Translator's note: The Vietnamese term *"nhân sinh,"* equivalent to "the *human condition,* " is defined as "the characteristics, key events, and situations which compose the essentials of human existence, such as birth, growth, emotionality, aspiration, conflict, and mortality."

[Source: https://en.wikipedia.org/wiki/Human_condition]

[89] Đức Lê Văn Duyệt Đại Tiên; Cơ Quan Phổ Thông Giáo Lý, the 15th day of the second month of Canh Tuất year (March 21, 1970).

accumulates more values in the collective: *As such, the collective values could be further and further improved, better shaped in the present and spiritually aspired to the future.*[90]

But how does one promote the synchronous progress in a collective? Đức Lê Đại Tiên taught: *It is the education that should play this important role in the fraternity stance.*[91]

In the art of contemporary leadership, to minimize the risks of inducing conflicts in an organization, the leadership team should be responsible for educating its organization via appropriate programs and formats.

For instance, the training program on organizational culture helps everyone learn how to behave and work together concordantly, scientifically, and effectively. This program makes everyone feels proud of him/herself when he/she treats their colleagues friendly, and feels ashamed when he/she aimlessly creates a discord in the organization.

This is not a fiction. Many multinational companies have had this kind of program. Based on such program, the managers in those companies train their employees through their daily tasks and achieve quite a lot of impressive results. Caodaists can certainly follow them and apply such programs to establish human fraternity in the mission for the Third Universal Salvation.

Đức Lý Giáo Tông did pose this problem to Cao Dai

---

[90] Đức Lê Văn Duyệt Đại Tiên, Cơ Quan Phổ Thông Giáo Lý, the 15th day of thesecond month of Canh Tuất year (March 21, 1970).

[91] Đức Lê Văn Duyệt Đại Tiên, Cơ Quan Phổ Thông Giáo Lý, the 15th day of the second month of Canh Tuất year (March 21, 1970).

disciples:

> *Human civilization is extremely advanced, mankind develops to the utmost. Although not yet being able to replace the Creator in the operation of the universe, mankind can implement and promote the infinite capacity, the transcendent wisdom that God bestowed to them. Looking inside the Caodaist organization, brothers and sisters, what do you think?*[92]

Of course, Đức Lý Giáo Tông wants that Caodaists altogether be awakened in God's favor to advance, at least to catch up with the world pace of progress—if not faster than that—to save mankind.

Đức Giáo Tông questioned further:

> *Being disciples of God, brothers and sisters, you are entrusted with the mission and receive the new method of Cao Dai, then at this moment where is your spiritual attainment of deliverance?*[93]

Then He Himself answered it:

> *Brothers and sisters in Cao Dai religion altogether (...), if you are not yet able to achieve the direct communion with God or attain the six transcendental powers or attain enlightenment right in this world, each of you must acquire the values of*

---

[92] Đức Giáo Tông Vô Vi Đại Đạo, Cơ Quan Phổ Thông Giáo Lý, the 17th day of the second month of Đinh Sửu year (March 25, 1997).

[93] Đức Giáo Tông Vô Vi Đại Đạo, Cơ Quan Phổ Thông Giáo Lý, the 17th day of the second month of Đinh Sửu year (March 25, 1997).

spiritual transcendence.[94]

The values of spiritual transcendence mentioned by Đức Giáo Tông are the virtuous values. Those values must be in our thought, speech, and action: *Each of you, brothers and sisters, must serve a virtuous example for mankind to look up, admire, and obey.*[95]

Progress is a motivation to promote human perfectionation in a natural way following the advances of society. Living in a world of extremely advanced wisdom, as identified by Đức Lý Giáo Tông, Caodaists have advantages to make great stride in work of merit, self-discipline, and meditation. But they should know how to use those advantages—and use them well.

Đức Lê Văn Duyệt Đại Tiên taught, *Progress means how to make people in society perfectionate naturally.*[96]

As such, human fraternity can be formed and developed consistently with the forward momentum of the entire world. When the progress reaches the point where everyone becomes used to live harmoniously, the virtuous spring will come and the history can no longer be reverted. If anyone still thinks about causing discord, he would have no courage to implement it. Why? Đức Lê Đại Tiên explains:

---

[94] Đức Giáo Tông Vô Vi Đại Đạo, Cơ Quan Phổ Thông Giáo Lý, the 17th day of the second month of Đinh Sửu year (March 25, 1997).

[95] Đức Giáo Tông Vô Vi Đại Đạo, Cơ Quan Phổ Thông Giáo Lý, the 17th day of the second month of Đinh Sửu year (March 25, 1997).

[96] Đức Lê Văn Duyệt Đại Tiên; Cơ Quan Phổ Thông Giáo Lý, the 15th day of the second month of Canh Tuất year (March 21, 1970).

Regarding any bad action against the principle of nature, no one dares to tempt it, not because of fearing of sins but because of the opposition to nature that he creates.[97]

5. GREETINGS TO THE FRATERNAL SPRING

In the New Year's Day the spring greetings are wonderful flavors of the fraternal atmosphere. It is not important whether the words are simple or cumbersome, genuine or superficial. It is also not important whether the content is repetitive or creative, realistic or illusory. The spring greeting is the art of choosing the words carefully to please each other. Thanks to this act of pleasing each other, the spring greetings become a unique means to express the peace-loving inclination.

Through invocation in Caodaism, divine beings bestowed us quite a few verses to greet the spring of humaneness, peacefulness, and progress. These spring greetings serve as a brief guide on how to successfully create the spring in human fraternity. For instance, Đức Lê Văn Duyệt Đại Tiên greeted as follows:

Wishing all, everybody,

Wishing men and women, elders and youngsters, distant and close,

Wishing you joyful scene and happy home,

---

[97] Đức Lê Văn Duyệt Đại Tiên; Cơ Quan Phổ Thông Giáo Lý, the 15th day of the second month of Canh Tuất year (March 21, 1970).

Wishing everyone concord and happiness.[98]

That is a greeting for the peaceful spring. With this soft greeting, let us remind each other that happiness and concord always stick together. To be concordant, it is necessary to bring happiness to each other in all circumstances. On the other hand, to enjoy happiness, it is necessary to preserve concord.

Along with greetings for the spring of peacefulness, let us revive the virtuous traditions of the Viet people from millennia and fit them to the contemporary world through the greetings to the spring of humaneness:

Wishing provinces, districts, villages, hamlets,

Wishing the Viet people domestic and overseas,

To love and help each other compassionately,

To avoid calamities and violence.

Wishing the entire mankind with no discernment,

To respect each other's life,

Wild or wise you are all human,

Poor or rich you breathe and live under the same sky.[99]

In a community, everyone differs from others with respect to their motive power, karmic condition, personality, preference, habit, etc.; however, they should

---

[98] Đức Lê Văn Duyệt Đại Tiên, Thánh tịnh Ngọc Minh Đài, the New Year's Day of Ất Mão year (Feb. 11, 1975).

[99] Đức Lê Văn Duyệt Đại Tiên, Thánh tịnh Ngọc Minh Đài, the New Year's Day of Ất Mão year (Feb. 11, 1975).

learn to intertwine in order for the community to exist. To intertwine, they should love each other. The humane greeting above reminds everyone to overcome all differences, to love and stick to each other, to resolve the common hardships together, and help each individual fulfill his/her own duties.

Besides the humane spring greeting for the Viet people and the entire mankind, we also reserve a humane spring greeting for all the religious leaders in Vietnam as well as worldwide.

This special greeting from Đức Lê Văn Duyệt Đại Tiên expresses divine beings' expectations for the dignitaries, missionaries, and religious leaders in the Great Way for the Third Universal Salvation:

> *Wishing the religious leaders*
>
> *Entrusted by God to perform spiritual leadership,*
>
> *To educate and enlighten the people,*
>
> *To stop discriminating the self from nonself, right from wrong.*
>
> *The Great Way has multiple branches,*
>
> *It is like multiple forms of cake made up of rice from the same crock.*
>
> *The spiritual differs from the temporal, due to human condition,*
>
> *Yet, both are created by one God only.*[100]

---

[100] Đức Lê Văn Duyệt Đại Tiên, Thánh tịnh Ngọc Minh Đài, the New Year's Day of Ất Mão year (Feb. 11, 1975).

This spring greeting calls for the leaders to work together to eliminate the discriminatory stigma in the public, which is the selfish way of thinking that is always filled with prejudice, leading to discriminatory treatment and hindering all efforts to restore humaneness.

Đức Cao Triều Phát taught this:

What is called golden rules and standards, i.e., the dogma that framed humans in selfishness, the factor that built up these paths of hindrance and partition, if they are not eliminated by the mighty arms, the rivers of humaneness could not coincide and unite into the sea.[101]

Religious leaders, regardless of their ranks, are always in good position to eliminate the rootless factors, contribute to the restoration of humaneness in the community or society under their leaderships, and guide the people in that community back to the common origin of mankind.

In addition to the greetings for peaceful and humane spring, the greeting for progressive spring reveals expectations for the innovation, especially the innovation in the cultivator's outcomes:

Wishing the cultivator to be soon enlightened,

Treat each other with self-control,

Forge the heart with virtues and radiance,

---

[101] Đức Cao Triều Phát ,Minh Lý Thánh Hội, the 23rd day of the fourth month of Kỷ Dậu year (June 07, 1969).

Care more on morality and less on worldly matter.[102]

Self-control is the key to progress. Implementing this key, we can recognize that the entire advance in fraternity stance lies on the concrete outcomes of the spiritual way to deliverance as well as of the temporal way to harmony:

Wishing the esoteric practitioners,

Wishing the cultivators of heart,

To master the seven emotions and six senses,

To block evil invasion and trouble from the outside.

Wishing the missionaries on behalf of God,

Wishing the preachers of the doctrine,

To hold each other's hands to form the bridge,

And establish fraternity to build the world harmony.[103]

For this Tết, let us greet each other with these fraternal wishes, then together we will transform those noble expectations into effective outcomes of reality.

6. CONCLUDING NOTES

In the spring of Bính Dần year (1926), God advised

---

[102] Đức Lê Văn Duyệt Đại Tiên, Thánh tịnh Ngọc Minh Đài, the New Year's Day of Ất Mão year (Feb. 11, 1975).

[103] Đức Đại Tiên Lê Văn Duyệt, Thánh tịnh Ngọc Minh Đài, the New Year's Day of Ất Mão year (Feb. 11, 1975).

the Caodaists: *Teach each other the word harmony.*[104] This sincere advice was retrieved from a copy of *Thánh Ngôn Hiệp Tuyển*[105] whose pages already turned yellow with age.

Almost ninety spring seasons have passed since the initiation of the Great Way, and another spring is arriving. Outdoors, the spring spectacles are up and coming to remind us that the culmination of heaven-earth favor for the mission of the Third Salvation has been fully set. *The only missing factor in this mission is human fraternity, human fraternity again and again.*

Today, let each of us be determined to create the three-legged stance of humaneness, peacefulness, and progress right within the scope of our specific religious activities. Tomorrow, the spring in fraternity will come to Caodaist community, to Vietnam land, and to human heart all over.

Sài Gòn, the Winter's End of Quý Tỵ Year (2013)

Speech delivered at the Organization for Preaching the Doctrine of the Great Way on the 15ᵗʰ day of the 12ᵗʰ month of Quý Tỵ year (January 15, 2013)

---

[104] *Thánh Ngôn Hiệp Tuyển (The Collection of Holy Teachings)* Vol. 1, Séance on Feb. 20, 1926, i.e., *Thánh Ngôn Hiệp Tuyển*, 1ˢᵗ Ed. (Đinh Mão year), Tam Thanh printing house (Đa Kao, Sài Gòn) in 1928, consisting of 101 pages, dimension 14.8 x 22.2 centimeters.

[105] Translator's note: It is the *Collection of Holy Teaching*, original version.

THE CHORUS BETWEEN
SPRING HEART & SPRING SCENE

As cold wind blows at the end of the lunar year, the Viet people start preparing for the coming spring season. In the countryside, they gather banana leaves, sweet rice, onions, and tuber plants. They make rice cakes and pickles. In the urban areas, everyone hastily wraps up the year-end works to enjoy the leisure of the Tết[106] festival.

In the warm atmosphere of the Vietnamese New Year's Day, the religions imported from other cultures also participate in Vietnamese cultural and traditional spring climes. Buddhist pagodas usually open for visitors from all over the world to come and venerate the Buddhas, pick the fortune buds, and/or consult the oracles in the New Year's Eve. Catholic parishes organize Holy Mass in the night of New Year's Eve as well as on New Year's Day; On the second day of the year an additional Mass is organized in the parish cemetery to commemorate the ancestors and give the adherents the chance to burn incense sticks at the graves of the deceased.

As for Caodaism—a religion that was founded on Vietnam land and built from the national soul and national essence of Vietnam—spring is an attractive and intimate topic on religious instructions to the public. Every Vietnamese can be empathetic with Caodaism while

---

[106] Translator's note: Tết is Vietnamese New Year's Day, which is the first day of the lunar calendar.

turning the pages of holy teaching filled with literature and poetry on the spring topic. These are not the rhythmic verses describing spectacles or sentiments to entertain the readers in the new year holidays; instead, the religious instructions on the spring topic play a special role in the vivid demonstration of the spiritual way in human world. Moreover, God—the founder of Cao Dai Great Way—also taught us as follows:

> *The method that optimizes your capacity and characteristics to protect the rights of human status is entirely set in the meaning of spring, because spring symbolizes for warmness, for your Master's love, and for the life everlasting along with the universe.*
>
> *Therefore, children, you should refer to such meaning to maintain the moderation and equanimity of your spirit, to nurture the perfect good and perfect enlightenment of the true nature that your Master bestowed to each of you.*[107]

1. THE HARMONY BETWEEN SPRING HEART AND SPRING SCENE

Reading Cao Dai teaching on the spring topic, we seem to distinguish two types of spring: an ordinary spring of the outside spectacles, namely the spring scene, and a miraculous spring of the inner, or the spring heart.

However, spring scene without spring heart is

---

[107] Đức Cao Đài Thượng Đế, Thánh Thất Nam Thành, the Lunar New Year's Day of Canh Tuất year (Feb. 06, 1970).

merely an impermanent and deciduous spectacle, whereas spring heart without spring scene is merely the subliminal perception of the cultivators. To appreciate a meaningful spring, there should be the harmony between spring heart of human spirit and spring scene of nature.

Đức Giáo Tông Đại Đạo Thái Bạch Kim Tinh taught the following:

> *Spring is the scene at culmination of heaven-earth favor,*
>
> *Only with human fraternity, spring becomes the true spring.*
>
> *Years and months fly past endlessly.*
>
> *Knowing the spring, you can enjoy the splendid spring climes.*[108]

Spring is the true spring only if there is the coordination between spring scene and spring heart. When heaven-earth initiates the spring scene, humans respond to it with the spring in their hearts. When the spring heart in humans is triggered, spectacles of heaven-earth also support it and look more beautiful, more joyful to humans.

Such coordination forms a sequence of consecutive stages of initiation and response between spring heart and spring scene. When spring heart initiates, spring scene responds, and vice versa; the process keeps developing rhythmically through the high and low pitches of different chords formed between human heart and spectacular

---

[108] Đức Giáo Tông Vô Vi Đại Đạo, Cơ Quan Phổ Thông Giáo Lý, the 29th day of the 12th month of Mậu Ngọ year (Jan. 27, 1979).

creatures. Such initiation-and-response of spring heart and spring scene would produce magnificent harmonies between heaven-earth and mankind. These harmonies form the chorus that is named the spring.

In a choir, singers are divided into different parts based on their vocal ranges: *soprano* is the highest of the four standard singing voices; *alto* is below the highest range and above tenor; *tenor* is a singing voice between alto and basso, usually it is the highest of the ordinary adult male range; and *basso* is the lowest of the four standard singing voices.

This is a type of music originated from Pythagoreanism of ancient Greece, and has been well developed in European cultures. Vietnamese people usually dislike it when they listen to each part singing the melodies (of a chorus) separately. Each part sounds bad in its own way! The high-pitched part sounds whistling, the low-pitched one sounds very dull, yet another one is so monotonous that it does not sound melodic at all; not to mention the counter melody in opposite diacritical tones of Vietnamese lyric—for example, instead of "văn hiến Tiên Rồng" they make it sound like "văn hiền tiền rống," causing conflictions with the leading part!

Nevertheless, when all the parts assemble together, i.e., sing simultaneously under the conductor's guide, a miracle immediately occurs. All the previous confusing contradictions turn out to harmoniously complement each other; the leading part blows the soul into the supporting ones, while the supporting parts give vitality to the leading one. All of these concurrent sounds become the harmonious chords to create the emotional power of the song in the audience's heart.

The miracle that a chorus demonstrates—see how simple it is—lies in a single word: *harmony*. Similarly, the miracles of the spring only happen in the harmony between spring heart and spring scene. If we successfully live in such harmony, our individual life can be described by the following holy statement of Đức Giáo Tông Đại Đạo Thái Bạch Kim Tinh:

Spring exists, so do spectacles and emotions,

Heart exists, so do the Way and the everlasting life,

Spring is the virtue of God,

Contemplate the spring to appreciate the heart of nature.[109]

2. SPRING SCENE

As flowers bloom and buds sprout, the spectacle becomes beautiful and life flares up in vitality. Under the invisible brushstrokes of the Creator's affection, spring scene in this world is really the masterpiece of art for mankind to contemplate. Nevertheless, God is modernizing the way of appreciating the spring scene that mankind has been accustomed for millennia, to let them look further into their heart and envision the virtuous spring of the future. God Master taught:

Children, in general, spring scene has little

---

[109] Đức Giáo Tông Đại Đạo Thái Bạch Kim Tinh, Cơ Quan Phổ Thông Giáo Lý, the 29th day of the 12th month of Mậu Ngọ year (Jan. 27, 1979).

*meaning! As flowers are freshly blooming, you
cosset their branches, water and feed their roots,
smell the fragrance of their pistils. Why don't you
feed the Way perennial root, cosset to make the true
heart fresh and brilliant to foretaste the miraculous
scent of the Way expressed from your own inner?*[110]

Does it mean that Caodaism wishes to "religionize"
the spring and "propagate" a religious atmosphere into
every ordinary matter of mankind?

Absolutely not. Caodaism is striving to steer clear of
a real tragedy for this planet. Our entire mankind has been
living in a catastrophic winter in this degenerate era—
earthquakes, tsunamis, hurricanes, floods, droughts,
epidemics, wars, and terrorism further and further spread
throughout the five continents—and Caodaism brings to
mankind in general, to the Viet people in particular, the new
conceptions of the everlasting principles of the virtuous
spring.

Happiness would not exist in life if mankind are
contented with the brief joyfulness coming from the outside
factors. All spring spectacles, regardless of how splendid
they are, will later yield to the scorching summer sun and
the autumn's heavy rain in this impermanent life. No
wonder why many poets penned the sorrowful spring
verses:

Spring shows among the apricot blossoms

The full figure of Spring Queen in her deciduous

---

[110] Đức Chí Tôn Thượng Đế, Thánh Thất Nam Thành, the Lunar New
Year's Day of Canh Tuất year (Feb. 06, 1970).

days.[111]

In the sorrow of these verses, even if Spring Queen comes with the spring scene, it is merely the impermanent beauty. Therefore, Đức Liễu Tâm Chơn Nhơn Huỳnh Ngọc Trác warned this:

> *As for religious leaders, they must foresee and foreknow. Do not focus to spring scene, but do focus to spring heart, because spring scene is just a clime that changes with the operating mechanism of Creation. Spring scene is the temporary break of the chilly winter, to restart and rearrange for the new year's clime. Then the spring gets to its end, gradually transforming into summer, autumn, winter, alternatively and consecutively in the operation of the heaven wheel, in the endless cycle. Cause is followed by effect, then effect reverts to cause. How many people in this world enjoy an everlasting spring and successfully avoid the summer sun scorch, the winter frostbite?*[112]

Fortunately, from a very long time ago, the Viet ancestors made the spring scene of nature become the spring culture based on the national spirit and national essence of the Viet people. Ancient Vietnamese paid sincere homage to the sacred atmosphere of the first moments of a new year, because such atmosphere, boldly in spiritual colors, could wake the humane values in human

---

[111] Poet Bùi Giáng (1926-1998).

[112] Đức Liễu Tâm Chơn Nhơn Huỳnh Ngọc Trác, Thánh Thất Bình Hòa, the 26th day of the 12th month of Đinh Mùi year (Jan. 25, 1968).

hearts. Thanks to this homage, appreciation of traditional Tết lies in the warm and close-knit atmosphere of families, clans, villages, and not simply in the superficial games for enjoyment.

It would be wonderful if we had had a chance to live a Tết under Kings Lý and Trần, or in an epoch when the Three Religions[113] were still highly revered in the Viet society, so as to experience the spring scene carrying the real essence of the spring heart, with the Viet spirit especially bold. Yet, over the previous one hundred years, the appreciation of traditional Tết has been gradually fading along with the moral traditions. Vietnamese literature recorded "The Calligrapher" by poet Vũ Đình Liên (1913-1996) that depicts the image of a calligrapher fading through the Tết of pre-wartime in North Vietnam:

> *Peaches blossom this year*
>
> *Again the calligrapher came*
>
> *To the crowded town*
>
> *With his pen and ink.*
>
> *(...)*
>
> *There the calligrapher sits*
>
> *Passersby are ignorance*
>
> *Script covered by leaves*

---

[113] Translator's note: The Three Religions in Asia are Buddhism, Taoism, and Confucianism.

Dusted with rain...[114]

The forgetting that the North Vietnamese in early twentieth century had for the old calligrapher, who sat on the sidewalk of a crowded town in the Tết events, is a lamentable alarm for the modern Viet society. Not only has Confucianism been forgotten but also all the cultural and spiritual values as well as the moral traditions in life have been degraded.

As a consequence, the Viet people little by little tend to materialize the spring and degrade the Tết traditions. They spend a lot of money on food catering and enjoyments in Tết's days, creating excessive wastes of food in the first days of every year just to obtain good luck. Meanwhile, the moral values and cultural basis of the Tết traditions are neglected.

The Tết traditions and the way people appreciate the spring have been "denatured," and the delicate spring scene of nature has become a vulgar spring scene that humans created from their greediness in consuming their own resources. Spring is no longer fulfilled with its sacred look; instead, it is sunk in the cycle of warm-cold, joyful-sorrowful life dramas of this impermanent world.

3. SPRING HEART

Behind the jubilant and brilliant features of spring scene, we can always see those of spring heart in all beings

---

[114] Translator's note: Excerpted from the English translation by Gordon Tran, ACG Senior College in Auckland (http://movingwordsnz.weebly.com/gordon-tran.html).

and in mankind. Though the spring heart features differ from those of spring scene, they are as jubilant and brilliant as those of spring scene, or even much more than the latter, because spring heart is the true vitality of spring scene.

Đức Hưng Đạo Đại Vương taught the following:

Autumn ends, winter fades, then spring comes. Like that, sun and moon, yin and yang follow one another along with the Creator's moving wheel, all beings circulate together with the destined cycle. When spring arrives, trees and plants took off the brown layer of dead leaves to put on a fresh green color. Though vegetations are unconscious beings, the miraculous potential that God bestowed to each of them self-transforms in their subconsciousness to receive the spring weather and harmonize with all creatures.

Any time the spring arrives, every being self-transforms accordingly with the evolution law, from inferior to superior, from young to old, from a naive newborn, little by little his intelligence is mature along with the growing of his body, then he becomes an elder with gradual health degradation to turn back to the infancy stage of the past and surrender to the growing spring of the youth.

The law on birth, growth, maturation, and reproduction does not wait for anyone specifically, the impartial rule of heaven-earth does not apply to any creature particularly. Any time when winter fades and spring comes, each person has had a human body enclosing personal thoughts, an intelligent brain, and the discernment of right-wrong, good-bad, righteous-devilish, as well as wise-wild. Regardless of whether he/she is a minimum-wage worker or a wise intellectual, whether he/she likes or dislikes, his/her thoughts are still twinkling when the spring arrives. It is understandable that rich and famous people with excessive resources race each other to enjoyments; but as for the poor and needy people, living paycheck to paycheck, even though they want to forget or ignore the spring arrival, they still find some excitement in their heart. [115]

The burgeoning in plants is an expression of spring heart in the subconsciousness of vegetation. The excitement in people when spring comes is an expression of spring heart in humans. Yet, spring is not just that. Đức Thánh Trần stated this:

Spring comes and fits inside everybody,

Rich or poor, fine or coarse, all enjoy it;

Is the spring only that much,

If the debt to country has been forgotten? [116]

Man, along with heaven and earth, is one of the three persons of the universe, namely the Universal Triad in

---

[115] Đức Hưng Đạo Đại Vương, Minh Lý Thánh Hội, the third day of the first month of Canh Tuất year (Feb. 08, 1970).

[116] Đức Thánh Trần, i.e., Đức Hưng Đạo Đại Vương, Minh Lý Thánh Hội, the third day of the first month of Canh Tuất year (Feb. 08, 1970).

oriental theologies. The universe has the Way, mankind has the heart. This heart is essentially the permanent and everlasting spring in humans, and each of us has the mission to spread those permanent and everlasting seeds into the world. God taught the following:

Being one in the Universal Triad,

Being myriad in the Principle of Monad

Children! You are entrusted by God

The miraculous machine of Creation.

It includes the entire universe

It includes individual forms of all beings

It includes the everlasting spring

Coming to this world to recruit the soul of all beings.

Your Master assigns you a two-way mission

One departs from, the other returns to Him.

Regardless of the location: south, north, east, west

Ancient or modern, man and all beings are assigned by Him.[117]

As human heart has been covered by the six

---

[117] Đức Chí Tôn, Cơ Quan Phổ Thông Giáo Lý, the 30th day of the 12th month of Quý Sửu year (Jan. 22, 1974).

desires[118] and seven emotions[119] after undergoing innumerable past lives—due to the transmutation through many reincarnation cycles—this spring heart cannot self-reveal and humans have to find it, restore it, and rekindle it in their inner. God taught the following:

> *It is not only in one spring season following the summer, autumn, and winter, two spring seasons or hundreds, thousands of spring seasons expressing in brief periods, but it should be the same in every season; children, if you should always forge your heart to be fresh and pure, warm and gentle, with no hate, no ignorance, no ambition, you are certainly close to your Master....*
>
> *So, you live in the permanent spring, everlasting, indefinite, and endless in time. That is the spring of virtue. As for the spring of this year, your Master only expects that you, children, clean up your heart to welcome the spring and, children, remember that it should be the everlasting spring of virtue.[120]*

Therefore, spring heart is the inner state that is *fresh and pure, warm and gentle, without hate, without ignorance, without ambition* and inside everybody. The season of spring heart will come to our inner if we replace

---

[118] Translator's note: The six desires or sensual attractions are color, form, carriage, voice or speech, texture (smoothness or softness), and features.

[119] Translator's note: The seven emotions are joy, sorrow, love, hatred, pleasure, anger, and fear.

[120] Đức Chí Tôn, Thánh Thất Nam Thành, the Lunar New Year's Day of Canh Tuất year (Feb. 06, 1970).

the profane states of the six attractions and the seven emotions by these beautiful states of spring heart. God taught the following:

Spring is the Way, the Way bestowed by God

The Way is spring, the peaceful spring of nature

Enjoy the spring means enjoy the inner heart

The harmonious climes, the peaceful mankind and creatures.[121]

4. SPRING OF CHILDHOOD

We have seen many times the spring scene through the masterpiece of colorful spring in nature. We have also seen quite a few times the spring heart when our own inner state is *fresh and pure, warm and gentle, without greed, anger, or ignorance.* Now, as for the chorus between these two springs, can we prove its presence? Đức Diêu Trì Kim Mẫu questioned us: *Heaven-earth is gleaming*

Vegetation is charming

Landscape is stunning

Where to find the chorus of peacefulness

For predestined men[122] to avoid stormy

---

[121] Đức Chí Tôn, Cơ Quan Phổ Thông Giáo Lý, the 30th day of the 12th month of Giáp Dần year (Feb. 10, 1975).

[122] Translator's note: Predestined men (or original men) are superior spirits returning to this world to amass more credits and virtues by serving and supporting all beings. Progressive men (or evolutionary men) are those created through the material evolution by gradually developing from minerals to plants, animals, and humans. Differences

journeys?[123]

In the childhood stage of each person's lifetime, we did live in such seemingly endless *chorus of peacefulness.* And God revived that chorus in our memory:

Children, do you recall your childhood spring,

A springtime in concert with nature?[124]

At birth, human nature is still holy and innocent. In theology, that state of human nature is called *xích tử chi tâm* (the newborn's heart). This newborn's heart is still clear and radiant, not yet stained with worldly dust; it is also the spring heart innately given by God to create the natural spring in the human body.

Throughout the childhood, when a person has not yet been controlled by his/her own six desires and seven emotions, not yet known of worries, sundry thoughts, clinging to self, greed, anger, and ignorance, he/she has not been tied to any kind of suffering, grief, or karma-cause; therefore, he/she lives tranquilly, easily, and freely in the innocent world of children.

That is the spring heart of childhood every one of us experienced. Such spring heart never opposes the nature outside as it always harmonizes with the outside, always

---

between original man and progressive man are merely their past evolutionary achievements; but these do not determine future developmental progresses.

[123] Đức Diêu Trì Kim Mẫu, Hườn Cung Đàn, the 29th night to the New Year's Day of Quý Mão year (Jan. 24 - 25, 1963).

[124] Đức Chí Tôn, Cơ Quan Phổ Thông Giáo Lý, the New Year's Eve of Quý Sửu year (Jan. 22, 1974).

observing this principle: *Obeying the Celestial Law means alive; violating it, dead.*

Thanks to this harmony between spring heart and spring scene, children feel every season is beautiful as the spring, and every day is happy as Tết New Year's Day. That is a marvelous state of life, exactly like what God described:

> *In particular, human beings have consciousness,*
>
> *A glorious spring of victory*
>
> *Never mind summer or winter*
>
> *Like in the thirty-six heavens they enjoy the spring leisurely.*[125]

In summer it is very hot; but kids still happily play under the sun at noontime, while adults feel tired and complain about the suffocating and sultry atmosphere.

In autumn it is raining; but kids still comfortably take a bath under the rain for long hours, while adults melancholically lament with coughs, colds, and flu after getting a little soaked in the rain along the way.

In winter it is windy, misty, and cold; but kids still buoyantly play throughout the chilly evenings, while adults slump in thick sweatshirts.

Then in spring, this is the only season that adults feel happy despite all worries in preparing for the Tết festival of their immediate as well as distant families; of course, for

---

[125] Đức Chí Tôn, Cơ Quan Phổ Thông Giáo Lý, the New Year's Eve of Quý Sửu year (Jan. 22, 1974).

kids this must be the most cheerful season.

Adults seem to have something to grieve about in every season, while kids are always happy. Children enjoy the infinite happiness in the middle of an empty universe, and their happiness is not due to any material reason. With such happiness everyone dares to rewrite Descartes's famous quote to indicate his/her childhood: *I enjoy, therefore I am!*[126]

It turns out that childhood in every human is the stage of *Never mind summer or winter; Like in the thirty-six heavens they enjoy the spring leisurely.* Growing up, why can humans no longer live in these happy inner states? God explained:

> *Due to material desire, karmic effects are created*
>
> *Due to deviation from the origin, returning hints are lost*
>
> *Through countless seasons of autumn rain and summer sun*
>
> *Golden body[127] gets exiled in profane body.*[128]

Material desire—meaning the desire, either direct or indirect, for everything belonging to the material realm—is forever the cause of this tragedy. This material desire in our inner is so scary, because it frequently controls us though

---

[126] René Descartes (1596-1650) stated: I think, therefore I am. / *Je pense, donc je suis.*

[127] Translator's note: the Vietnamese term "Kim Thân" literally means the body made of gold, alluding to the spiritual body.

[128] Đức Chí Tôn, Cơ Quan Phổ Thông Giáo Lý, the 30th day of the 12th month of Quý Sửu year (Jan. 22, 1974).

we can hardly recognize it.

If ordinary people are fond of money and riches, we say that they are controlled by material desire. That is right! But if religious people stubbornly cling to a single word or phrase in other people's speech, they are also controlled by material desire. Why?

Linguists state that speech is the material cover of thought. When we cling to speech, we cling to this material cover, stick to this material cover, and such action is actually an action of material desire; in a more popular language, it is called fond of quarrel.

Thus, whether it is fond of money or fond of quarrel (for instance), all of them are different forms of the demoniac haze of material desire. Little by little that demon entices humans to leave the innocent and pure world of newborn's heart, and gradually get lost in the obscure jungle of karmic effects.

At birth, human heart has not yet been controlled by material desire. Recalling our childhood, we can understand the source of this happiest stage in our life. Part of this happiness must be from the innocent and pure nature of the newborn's heart, but the more important part is from the ability of the newborn's heart to harmonize with the spectacles of heaven-earth.

When harmony exists between the two factors heart and scene, the true spring appears in our life like a marvelous chorus. On the other hand, if either one of these two factors is missing, the spring is just the spring for someone else and not for ourselves.

Indeed, even when the spring heart fills up our inner

with warm, gentle thoughts, if that spring heart does not harmonize with the spring scene of nature we might get sick by just a cool breeze of the Tết climes and have to take a whole lot of different medications—such as antibiotics—then the spring seems no longer enjoyable in such miserable circumstances!

Considering these troublesome matters, people lamentably regret: "Alas! I'm so sorry for my newborn's heart! As it gets lost, how can I regain it?"

Well, it is fortunate for those who ask such a question in this Third Salvation![129] It is the new method of Cao Dai that teaches mankind how to restore the newborn's heart and revive the innocent and holy nature. Otherwise, "the old woodman" named Đông Phương Lão Tổ would not mention the virtuous task of his spiritual mission in the south as follows:

> *The old woodman enjoys the scene of wind and lakes*
>
> *He chops wood, clears forest, cuts karmic links*
>
> *In exchange for the precious rice, to feed the newborn*

---

[129] Translator's note: Caodaism has its own historical viewpoint to explain the historic progress of mankind, which can be divided into three eras: The First Era (about 4,300 years ago), the Second Era (lasted for thirty centuries, from 2000 B.C. to about 1000 A.C.), and the Third Era (from the nineteenth century to present). At the end of each era, God disseminates the Way (the Dao) into this world to save mankind. The Great Way for the Third Universal Salvation was initiated when God founded Caodaism in South Vietnam in Bính Dần year (1926).

And sow the virtuous seeds in the South land.[130]

This virtuous task comes from another profound meaning of the spring, which is: The Third Salvation in the degenerate age of Dharma.[131]

5. SPRING OF THE DEGENERATE AGE OF DHARMA

Discussing the dogma in the spring, God emphasized a very special meaning:

In the Third Salvation your Master initiates the Dharma

To extend the collection of predestined people

On the river of ignorance the boat of wisdom is ready

For the wise to return to the home of Saints and Immortals.[132]

Where is the spring in the above verses?

---

[130] Đông Phương Lão Tổ, Thiên Lý Đàn, the 23rd day of the 12th month of Giáp Thìn year (Jan. 25, 1965).

[131] Translator's note: The term Dharma has many translations. By combining the English meaning of these words: teachings, truths, facts and natural laws, then emphasizing the definition depending on the nature of the subject being discussed, one can usually understand the meaning of dharma in each instance. For example, the meaning of *dharma* in the Triple Gem's "Buddha, Dharma and Sangha" includes all of these: teachings, truths, facts and natural laws. (Source: http://buddhismteacher.com/dharma.php).

[132] Đức Chí Tôn, Cơ Quan Phổ Thông Giáo Lý, the New Year's Eve of Quý Sửu month (Jan. 22, 1974).

We can find the answer from God in another invocation: *Your Master initiates the Third Universal Salvation for you, children, and for the entire mankind, like the spring coming to all creatures.*[133]

The spring of the degenerate age of Dharma is the boat of wisdom, namely the Great Way for the Third Universal Salvation, that God already anchored on the river of ignorance to wait for all beings and ship them to the awakening shore. Therefore, Đức Giáo Tông Đại Đạo advised that the predestined people, who cultivate the Spiritual Way, should implement successfully this sacred spring to save themselves and save others:

> *From the fairy mount, holy land, ever-spring heaven,*
>
> *So many predestined people get lost on the worldly land.*
>
> *Holding God's favor in hands,*
>
> *Be persistent in daily practice of the God-Way.*
>
> *Appreciate the wonder of natural sight,*
>
> *Enjoy the quietude of meditating mind.*
>
> *Nothing is real beyond the spirit of light,*
>
> *Do not constrain it with worldly ties.*
>
> *Countless passengers cross the worldly dock,*
>
> *Being undulated with the tidal grief in this world.*
>
> *Awakened people foretaste the spiritual scent,*
>
> *Why do you waste time and effort like the profane?*

---

[133] Đức Chí Tôn, Cơ Quan Phổ Thông Giáo Lý, the New Year's Eve of Giáp Dần year (Feb. 10, 1975).

134

The Third Universal Salvation is a sacred and everlasting spring that God brings to the entirety of mankind in this winter of eradication mechanism. Only in that spring, mankind can hope for a future, and the Viet people can establish the paradise on Earth for all beings.

It is due to the cultivation of this sacred spring that quite a few messiahs from previous universal salvations had incarnated as Vietnamese in the third era, to share the ups and downs in the history of the Viet people and pave the road for the historical mission of the Viet people. Caodaist Pioneers spoke their mind as follows:

For the sacred and infinite spring

We incarnated in the world to adorn this country

Making plants and flowers show their vivid colors

So everyone participates in the spring happily.

Amid the world filled with spring scent

Only Vietnam feels despondent

As its entire land is consistent

But the North and South people are divergent.

In front of the desk blurred by incense smoke

New Year's Eve firecrackers are echoing

Under the sky of scattering stars

---

134 Đức Giáo Tông Đại Đạo, Minh Đức Tu Viện, the 25th day of the first month of Giáp Dần year (Feb. 16, 1974).

Spring breeze turns old affections cold.

Burn the sandalwood to warm the affections

Pick the sacred penbrush to sketch a harmonious stretch

Spring idea is simple but profound

So everybody can enjoy the radiant spring heart.

That spring heart is bestowed by God

To everybody and is everlasting

Alas, the world! Whether you mourn or laugh

Tend your hands to grip the boat of altruistic love.

Be humble to hold up your home faith

Forge yourself with benevolence and righteousness

Toward God, the country, and the people

In time of trouble or danger, self-sacrifice to help others.[135]

Đức Liễu Tâm Chơn Nhơn Huỳnh Ngọc Trác taught this:

With spring heart, humans become liberated, selfless, non-clinging, tolerant, and forgiving. With spring heart, humans have loving-kindness from the bottom of their heart and share it with all other people, all other creatures. With spring heart, one can lead this people away from declination, and

---

[135] Caodaist Pioneers, Thánh Thất Nam Thành, the Lunar New Year's Day of Canh Tuất year (Feb. 06, 1970).

guide mankind away from eradication. Such spring heart is Cao Dai Great Way that God entrusted to this people. Such invaluable treasure is waiting for the spring heart in humans to shine it up brilliantly.[136]

The presence of Caodaism in this world places mankind at the intersection of history between two turns:

- The first turn is that mankind must kindle the virtuous light in this world to transform the winter of the degenerate age of wisdom into the spring of the golden age of virtue.
- The second turn is that humans keep following their material desire to witness the karmic rife created by themselves to push mankind to the abyss of extermination.

Đức Cao Triều Phát taught the following:

Winter fades, spring comes. Multiple winters, multiple springs have passed, human fraternity has not yet been established, human heart has not yet been pacified. Mankind does not recognize and implement the truly virtuous way. Religion is still religion. Chaos is still chaos. Mankind will fade along with the winter, eradication mechanism will come along with the spring. That is an obvious argument in everyone's perception.[137]

---

[136] Đức Liễu Tâm Chơn Nhơn Huỳnh Ngọc Trác, Thánh Thất Bình Hòa, the 26th day of the 12th month of Đinh Mùi year (Jan. 25, 1968).

[137] Đức Cao Triều Phát, Thánh Thất Bình Hòa, the 26th day of the 12th month of Đinh Mùi year (Jan. 25, 1968).

On the second turn, *mankind will fade with the winter, and eradication will come with the spring*. We perceive the horrible spring scenes of the eradicating mechanism. Then, Caodaists must decisively guide mankind onto the first turn. They must wake up the spring heart in mankind and radiate it brilliantly as aspired by Đức Liễu Tâm Chơn Nhơn.

Therefore, any Caodaists who have not yet acquired the determination to save the world must at least be willing to serve mankind. Such determination and spirit would initiate and maintain the spring heart in everyone's inner; as a result, not only can we enjoy the spring but we can also gather sufficient momentum to implement the mission of obeying God to serve mankind.

We can find these points in one of the teachings given by God:

> *Spring is the Way operating and transforming in the dualistic world of visible-invisible, gain-loss; whereas the Spiritual Way is the mystic and everlasting spring. If you want to appreciate the spring, you should have the spring heart for the spring scene to be exposed. Once the spring heart is revealed, even when the circumstances are changing or grievous, your inner is still peacefully tranquil. With the tranquil and peaceful inner you can penetrate the dogma of the Way. With the penetration of the dogma of the Way, you can maintain the mystic power of obeying God to serve*

mankind.[138]

To successfully do so, our own inner should thrive with the spring heart, overfilling it with the fresh and cool breeze of tolerance and forgiveness, with the warm sunlight of loving-kindness, and with the gentle brushstrokes of harmony.

Once our inner is filled with spring heart, we will feel the natural need to kindly and generously give that spring to everybody around us, no matter who they are, friend or foe, intimate or distant. And this implementation is very similar to that of God's when He kindly and generously brought the spring to give to all beings in this world.

Despite the grievous circumstances and the changing world, your Master still reserves a warm spring with its natural beauty to offset the chilly winter, the scorching summer, and the melancholic autumn. Your Master comes to you, children, with a new spring. You should happily appreciate the spring, propagate the Way of your Master all over the world, widely sow the good seeds and preach the blessing to all his children, so they understand the dogmas of the Way and return to the principle of God-Man Union, in order to re-establish the saintly age of virtue.[139]

---

[138] Đức Chí Tôn, Cơ Quan Phổ Thông Giáo Lý, the transition time of the New Year's Eve to the New Year's Day of Bính Thìn year (Jan. 30 – 31, 1976).

[139] Đức Chí Tôn, Thiên Lý Đàn, the 29th day of the 12th month of Ất Tỵ year (Jan. 20, 1966).

6. APPRECIATING THE SPIRITUAL TASTE OF SPRING

As the beginning of a new year in this sentient world, spring brings to us a clear awareness of time, leading to an awareness of the impermanence, especially to those who have been worn and torn by the aging process of their physical bodies.

As for Caodaists, the awareness of time and impermanence reminds us of the thorough self-review of body and mind after a year living and practicing the Way in this world.

God taught this:

Spring is a repeating season in the process of birth, growth, maturation, and reproduction. Children, consider what should be removed and what should be brought to your upcoming journey so your trip will be completed with progress and purity.[140]

It is because of this self-review that we can appreciate the spiritual taste of spring. It sounds astonishing. Why does the self-review have functions on the appreciation of spring?

Đức Đông Phương Chưởng Quản explained it as follows:

The true meaning of the phrase 'appreciating the spring' should be tacitly revealed from one's inner.

---

[140] Đức Chí Tôn, Thánh Thất Nam Thành, the Lunar New Year's Day of Canh Tuất year (Jan. 06, 1970).

As for appreciating the spring apparently, it is only applied temporarily to people in this world. The reason is appreciating the spring apparently includes multiple facets but its aftermath makes everyone exhausted from body to mind. Not to mention the consequences such as sorrow, worries, fear, resentment after getting drunk.

As for appreciating the spring accordingly to the dogma, it is the self-review on one's own cultivation process throughout the past year. If he/she made progress in cultivating loving-kindness and selflessness by performing the Triple Work, he/she would feel delighted and open-hearted, full of love and compassion toward the unfortunate and homeless. With such tacit happiness manifesting from his/her inner, though he/she would sit back for the plain tea and simple sweet treats, his/her heart is so soothing and filled with hope, overflown with faith in divine beings'[141] *guide.*[142]

Thanks to the self-review after a year of practicing the Way especially the recognition of our own progress, our spring heart expresses harmonious chords with the spring scene. Indeed, the most significant happiness in a spring season is the recognition of the everlasting consequences that we have harvested in this impermanent world. Only with these consequences we are not struck with remorse for

---

[141] Translator's note: 'divine beings' is a general term to indicate all the Buddhas, immortals, saints, and deities.

[142] Đức Đông Phương Chưởng Quản, Thiên Lý Đàn, the New Year's Day of Kỷ Dậu year (Feb. 16, 1969).

a human life as the time passes. Divine beings taught:

Winter fades, landscape turns into spring

Spring has bloomed on the apricots multiple times

Multiple times the boat has departed from the port sacred

Sacred heart how many people have still cultivated?[143]

What do the above holy verses say? We can borrow Divine Mother's statement to explain them:

Children! Any time the spring comes, your Divine Mother's heart feels anxious. Spring comes, then spring goes. You welcome the spring by adding one more year to your age and you are about to reach the end of your missionary journey in the impermanent world. Your Divine Mother worries if you know such period is very precious, and if you note that the time passed never comes back. If you fail to make record of any turning point in the temporal or spiritual history, you merely continue the process of birth, growth, maturation, and reproduction forever, following the common law applied to all species in nature.[144]

No one dares to say exactly how many spring seasons he can see in his lifetime so he can postpone the

---

[143] *Thánh Ngôn Hiệp Tuyển (The Collection of Holy Teachings)*, Vol. 2, section *Thi Văn Dạy Đạo*, printed in 1970, page126.

[144] Đức Vô Cực Từ Tôn, Thánh thất Tân Định, the 6th day of the first month of Bính Ngũ year (Jan. 26, 1966).

cultivation of virtues and spiritual heart to later years. Neither can the salvation boat be anchored to wait forever, because waiting forever means the inability to save anyone. The boat of salvation has to leave the port of ignorance to return to the awakening shore at the destined time of the Creation mechanism.

7. CONCLUDING NOTES

Listening to the chorus between spring heart and spring scene in our inner, or recalling it from our childhood, we can discover a lot of miraculous dogmas that help us maintain the moderation and equanimity of our spirit, and as such, we can preserve the noble stance of mankind. We have forgotten our newborn's heart after passing the childhood stage, and even lost the spring chorus in the depths of consciousness. Who can help us regain the chorus between spring scene and spring heart? Only God can! And nowadays, with the new method of Cao Dai that God brought forth in this Third Salvation, we have in our hands the entire map to retrieve those miraculous harmonies.

Speech delivered at the
Organization for Preaching the Doctrine of the Great Way
on the 15th day of the 12th month of Bính Tuất year
(Jan. 14, 2006)

HAPPINESS
IN CAODAIST CONCEPTION

Happiness is a state of emotion in which humans reach the satisfaction for their wishes. In Vietnamese language, the word *niềm* (feeling) in the compound noun *niềm vui* (happiness) is to emphasize that such state of emotion is a state of the inner rather than one from the outside. In fact, Vietnamese people know that joyful spectacles never exist in the eyes of a sad person, and nothing seems sorrowful to happy people. Therefore, happiness is a state of the inner to express contentment due to the satisfaction of wishes, and the essence of happiness depends on the essence of the correlating wish.

Based on the experiences of ourselves as well as of other people, we can classify all human happiness in this world into two basic types: one helps raise human values, and the other lowers human dignity. In Caodaist terminology, the former is the *ethical happiness*, and the latter, the *unethical happiness*.

In ethical happiness, the more satisfaction one achieves the more sanctification he/she and other people attain. On the other hand, with unethical happiness, the more satisfaction one achieves, the more deluded and ignorant he/she becomes—and consequently the more easily he/she errs. Therefore, ethical happiness is the one that everyone should acquire, nurture, and develop in his/her inner as well as in the hearts of others; unethical happiness is the type that everybody must avoid.

1. ETHICAL HAPPINESS

Speaking of ethics is speaking of all the three values: truth, goodness, and beauty. Belonging to ethics must be everything concurrently right (truth), good (goodness), and aesthetic (beauty). These are also the three values of humaneness, i.e., the three fundamental values of human nature that, deeply in human subconsciousness, all people long for and admire.

Therefore, toward truth, goodness, and beauty, even a small progress can also bring enormous satisfaction to mankind. It explains why any person in this world would find wonderful happiness when he catches some tiny rays of truth, or experiences some virtuous thoughts, or performs some good deeds. Let us consider several examples:

First, we look at happiness from experiencing true verities (truth). Being students, many of us experienced indescribable happiness when we successfully solved a tough mathematics problem. Growing up and engaging in life, any time we could apply wisdom to successfully resolve the problems of human duties, similar happiness manifests. Thinkers around the world also experience such happiness any time they discover a truth that has still been hidden in nature or in society. As for religious devotees, any time they experience a spiritual power, a miraculous matter of faith, or conceive a transcendental content of dogma, they feel both their wisdom and spirit extraordinarily excited. These are candid and meaningful experiences about happiness in light of truth.

Second, we consider happiness from experiencing

good deeds (goodness). Any time we perform a good deed or help other people, we feel cheerful and lighthearted. Let us find what would happen if we expand the scope of our services. For instance, first we give food, clothes, and medications to the needy, and then gradually we move to the stage of transforming the troublemakers in society into useful people. The broader the scope of services, the harder the good deeds become, the more devoted we should be, and the more sacrifice to other people we should practice. But thanks to the scope expansion, the impact of the services would be broader and deeper, the number of people receiving services is also augmented, and our happiness is multiplied. Thus, the level of sanctification we attain is due to the extent of our self-forgetfulness to sacrifice for the happiness of the mass public.

Third, we examine happiness from experiencing aesthetic realities (beauty). We can find such happiness when we humble ourselves to bring glory to other people in the ethical light, or when we love our haters and use loving-kindness to treat their hostility. This is an experience of the beauty, the transcendence in human personality; and those who recognize such beauty and transcendence in their own personality should be overjoyed.

These are some examples of ethical happiness from experiencing truth, goodness, and beauty. In fact, all three values of truth, goodness, and beauty usually manifest simultaneously. For example, applying loving-kindness to counteract hostility is not only an extremely aesthetic behavior, but it is also a deed extremely good and extremely right.

All ethical happiness implies the deep nature of

peacefulness. The word *peacefulness* in this context means *happiness due to attaining peace of heart*. Such peace cannot come from any outside factors and can only exist if we successfully maintain the equanimity in our own inner in all circumstances of life. Tranquil people do not let themselves be neither agitated nor excited by any factors from the outside. The more challenges such a person experiences through adversities, the more pure and holy happiness he feels, because those life hardships are the chances to forge and augment the values of humaneness in his personality.

The goal of Caodaism is *harmony in the temporal world, deliverance in the spiritual world*. In further details, this goal aims to concurrently lead mankind to the universal harmony and guide every individual back to the everlasting and holy realm called paradise in Christianity or nirvana in Buddhism. Peacefulness plays a significant role in both the individual and societal scopes.

Regarding the *individual* scope, peacefulness is an active motivator to liberate the inner from superficial desires. These desires do not exist on their own in the intrinsic essence of mankind. They are nothing else than the excited states of the inner under the influence of the outside. But if they show up endlessly, one manifests and adds to the other, they become an infinite storm of desire and prevents people from living in accord with their intrinsic essence.

Therefore, the more tranquil the inner is maintained, the more depressed the desires become, and the faster they dissipate. Once they disappear, the person will see the intrinsic essence; moreover, he will behold that this intrinsic essence is God, Buddha in perfect equanimity. Because peacefulness can only be in a tranquil heart, peacefulness is a powerful motivator for the evolution of human spirit to become Buddha and to mystically identify with God.

Regarding the *societal* scope, peacefulness is one of the factors in establishing the humane society, i.e., the peaceful society. In this scope, Cao Dai teaching pledges to *create the peaceful order to implement happiness in human condition.*[145],[146] Only when the societal order is an order originated from peacefulness, everyone can enjoy the true happiness and society really becomes the peaceful society.

But to create peaceful society, at first, there should be peaceful people. Those individuals are not cowards; instead, they already freed their heart from banal desires and achieved the inner peacefulness. Consequently, they can promote loving-kindness to engage in the adversities of life, relieve other beings from tribulations while maintaining and developing equanimity and peacefulness in their own heart and body. Saint Francis of Assisi (1182-

---

[145] Translator's note: The Vietnamese term "nhân sanh" is translated as "human condition" based on its definition as follows: The **human condition** is defined as "the characteristics, key events, and situations which compose the essentials of human existence, such as birth, growth, emotionality, aspiration, conflict, and mortality." This is a very broad topic which has been and continues to be pondered and analyzed from many perspectives, including those of religion, philosophy, history, art, literature, sociology, psychology, and biology. (Source: https://en.wikipedia.org/wiki/Human_condition).

[146] Đại Tiên Lê Văn Duyệt, Văn Phòng Cơ Quan Phổ Thông Giáo Lý Cao Đài Giáo Việt Nam, the 14th night to 15th day of the 2nd month of Canh Tuất year (March 21, 1970).

1226) quoted as follows: *Those who endure sickness and trial but still in peace, for the love of You, My Lord, they will be crowned.*[147]

2. UNETHICAL HAPPINESS

Unethical happiness consists of those not conforming to the three fundamental values of humaneness. They are neither right, good, nor aesthetic. They do not belong to the original nature. When God created mankind, He did not create these unethical characters. Then where did they come from?

According to Cao Đài teaching, human configuration consists of six organs that God created as the psychophysiological foundation for cognition. Those six organs are named the six senses,[148] comprising eye, ear, nose, tongue, body, and mind. They are *the six extremely important organs to form a human being in this world.*[149]

Analogous to the radar systems, the six senses are always ready to receive their corresponding factors of excitement from the outside. Such readiness creates the six desires at both levels of feeling and perception in humans. Those six desires are called the six sensual attractions, comprising sight, hearing, smell, taste, feature, and

---

[147] Source: https://en.wikiquote.org/wiki/Francis_of_Assisi. Vietnamese text: Norbertô Nguyễn Văn Khanh, ofm., *Thánh Phanxicô Átxidi, Con Người Của Hòa Bình.* http://www.ofmvn.org/linh-dao/thanh-phanxico/1378-. . ., 27-09-2013.

[148] Translator's note: Another name is the six roots of sensation.

[149] Đức Chí Tôn, "Đoạn Trừ Lục Dục", *Tam Thừa Chơn Giáo*, vol. 2. Séance on Nov. 08, 1961.

intellect.

If the soul can master the six senses and apply them in ethical matters, they would become the six miraculous powers to penetrate heaven and earth. On the other hand, if the soul cannot control the six senses, the six sensual attractions would blindly perform unethical matters and become *the six crooked paths*[150] that make humans fall interminably.

The extent and magnitude of satisfaction or dissatisfaction with those desires result in the seven emotional states in humans, which are joy, anger, sorrow, pleasure, love, hate, and fear.

These seven emotional states are called the seven emotions. They are all the excited states of the inner and manifest when people are affected by the outside factors with no equanimity of their inner. These states are temporary and unreal states, each of which can last for only a certain time after manifestation, before transforming into another state.

Unethical happiness is the happiness due to these seven emotional states. These types of happiness are generated and existed due to the six sensual attractions; hence, they are merely superficial excitements from the satisfaction of the psychophysiological desires in human subconscious instinct. In the language of psychoanalyst Sigmund Freud, those types of happiness are originated from *the impulses generated by physical structures,*[151] and

---

[150] Đức Chí Tôn, "Đoạn Trừ Lục Dục", *Tam Thừa Chơn Giáo*, vol. 2. Séance on Nov. 08, 1961.

[151] David Stafford-Clark, *What Freud Really Said: An Introduction to*

are the satisfaction for physical requirements in human mind.[152]

If people are happy because their *eyes* can see the gender beauty or the luxuriant nuances of riches, that is the happiness from *sight attraction.*

If people are happy because their *ears* can hear flattering words, praises, gossips, malicious talks, that is the happiness from *hearing attraction.*

If people are happy because their *nose* can smell flavors that generate bodily excitement, that is the happiness from *smell attraction.*

If people are happy because their *tongue* can taste delicious foods, that is the happiness from *taste attraction.*

If people are happy because their *body* is satisfied with other carnal desires, that is the happiness from *feature attraction.*

And if people are happy because their *mind* is satisfied with erroneous, debauched, or immoral thoughts, that is the happiness from *intellect attraction.*

The happiness of intellect attraction is the medium containing and nurturing the happiness of all other sensual attractions. Behind the ability of physiological perception of biological organs (for instance, the seeing of eyes, the hearing of ears) are the ability of psychological perception

---

His Life and Thought, Vietnamese translation by Lê Văn Luyện, Hà Nội: Nxb Thế Giới, 2011, pp. 151, 154.

[152] David Stafford-Clark, *What Freud Really Said: An Introduction to His Life and Thought*, Vietnamese translated by Lê Văn Luyện, Hà Nội: Nxb Thế Giới, 2011, pp. 151, 154.

of corresponding subconscious instincts (for instance, the seeing of subconscious instinct, the hearing of subconscious instinct).

The seeing or hearing of subconscious instinct arises in the mind through the activities of physical organs and nurtured by intellect attraction. It is those desires of subconscious instinct that are the most alarming part of the six sensual attractions.

With respect to the desires of subconscious instinct, one can control and master them, not by applying cognition or rationale, but by a long process of self-cultivation throughout his lifetime.

The task of guiding and providing people an effective method of self-cultivation cannot be succeeded by anyone but the religious devotees in this world. And it is also a reason why mankind needs religions.

3. LIVING WITH THE DAILY HAPPINESS

Ethical and unethical happiness, presented above in the language of Cao Đài teaching, are also discussed by other religions around the world in more or less different approaches but are fundamentally similar in content.

In Buddhism, the terms *peacefulness* (*an lạc*) and *pleasure* (*dục lạc*) are used in scriptures to indicate these two types of happiness.[153]

In Christianity, Saint Thomas Aquinas (1225-1274)

---

[153] Pháp Nguyện, *An Lạc Và Dục Lạc*, source: http://chuahaiquang.com.vn/ NewsDetails.aspx?_214=268. 25-9-2013.

distinguished *genuine happiness* from *superficial happiness*, as well as *good joy* from *evil joy*.[154]

In ordinary people, every happy feeling can belong to either one of these types of happiness or can be also a certain combination of these. Recognition of the essence of each type is significant in the formation of a person's own values. It requires from humans the habit of following, controlling, mastering, and selecting their own psychological states.

In daily activities, we can experience various happy feelings that seem to not belong to either one of the two types of happiness discussed above—for instance, the joy of graduation, the joy of finding a job, the joy of traveling, the joy of Tết arrival, etc.

In fact, the ethical and unethical nature of happiness does not lie in any event such as graduation, job acquiring, traveling, or Tết arrival; instead, it lies on the peacefulness level of the person's inner, i.e., the level of his/her self-control of the inner when he/she goes through that event.

For instance, if a student feels happy because the graduation is a fulfillment of his duties toward his family and a milestone of his own advance, that is an ethical happiness. It is so because, as Saint Thomas Aquinas defined, *happiness is the peaceful state of a person's inner after he achieves his goal*, i.e., a good deed.[155] But if the

---

[154] Priest Giuse Phan Tấn Thành, op., *Thần Học Niềm Vui 03: Chứng Nhân Niềm Vui*, http://2010menchuayeunguoi.blogspot.com/ 2010/01/ than-hoc-niem-vui-03-chung-nhan-niem.html. 25-9-2013.

[155] Priest Giuse Phan Tấn Thành, op., *Thần Học Niềm Vui 03: Chứng Nhân Niềm Vui*, http://2010menchuayeunguoi.blogspot.com/ 2010/01/ than-hoc-niem-vui-03-chung-nhan-niem.html. 25-9-2013.

student considers his graduation as the chance to quit forever his studying duties or a chance to celebrate and get drunk, then due to such impulsive excitement he loses self-control and causes harm to himself as well as to others, that is unethical happiness.

To recognize the ethical and unethical happiness in the inner, as well as to develop the former while avoiding the latter, humans really need help from religions. Each religion has its own methods appropriate to serve a variety of subjects.

Caodaism employs the method of Triple Work, comprising Work of Merit, Work of Virtue, and Work of Wisdom.

Work of Merit is to do the work beneficial to others with dedication and self-sacrifice, but without thinking of oneself or expecting any forms of appreciation, including the rewards bestowed by God and divine beings.

Đức Cao Triều Phát taught: *Be happy to serve others. Be proud of self-sacrificing for others.*[156]

Self-sacrificing for others is a happiness that not everyone in this world has a chance to experience, although such opportunities of sacrifice exist in every place and every time. Moreover, this happiness itself is an invaluable reward.

Work of Virtue is to forge one's own nature, cultivate one's own personality, and correct one's own behaviors in accord with the absolutely true, absolutely

---

[156] Đức Cao Triều Phát, Thánh thất Nam Thành, the Lunar New Year's Day of Ất Tỵ year (Feb. 02, 1965).

good, and absolutely aesthetic standards. With the assistance of commandments, Work of Virtue is the major method to follow, control, suppress, or remove unethical happiness. The basic efforts one should make in Work of Virtue are to master the six sensual attractions and the seven emotions, transforming them into ethical forces of the inner.

Work of Wisdom is to practice meditation. At the basic level, meditation is performed through the mental concentration while reciting prayers in worship sessions, in ritual ceremonies, and in other daily activities (such as reciting prayers before meals, before leaving home, after coming home, before going to bed, etc.). At the advanced level and in depth, meditation is implemented through the system of meditation methods belonging to the esoteric teaching of Caodaism. Meditation helps people frequently communicate with divine beings on one hand, while on the other hand—which is much more important—it helps people forge the equanimity and self-control of their inner. In other words, meditation is the solution to simultaneously terminate all the roots of unethical happiness and build solid foundation for the inner peacefulness.

Therefore, to live with the daily happiness, in Caodaist conception, is to *moralize* its essence, making it become the true, good, and aesthetic happiness if it has not yet attained these fundamental values of humaneness. This way of living itself is also an ethical happiness, an endless happiness in each person's life who is seeking to regain his original essence in the salvation grace of God.

Seminar presented at the

Inter-Religion Conference
Sep. 28, 2013
Phanxicô Đa Kao Monastery

References

Thiện Quang, *Tự Thắp Đuốc Mà Đi,* Tam Giáo Đồng Nguyên publisher, 2014.

Cao-Dai Great Way: The Grand Cycle of Esoteric Teaching, trans. Anh-Tuyet Tran, Cao-Dai Temple Overseas, 2015.

I-Ching or Book of Changes 3rd ed., trans. Richard Wilhelm and Cary F. Baynes, Bollingen Series XIX, Princeton NJ: Princeton University Press, 1967, 1st ed. 1950.

Dao De Jing: The Book of the Way, trans. Moss Roberts, University of California Press, 2004.

TUỆ QUANG BUDDHIST Multimedia Dictionary: http://www.phathoc.net/tu-dien-phat-hoc

Vietnamese-English Dictionary: http://www.lingvozone.com

Index

www.ingramcontent.com/pod-product-compliance
Lightning Source LLC
Chambersburg PA
CBHW061740020426
42331CB00006B/1302